Tom Ferris

IRISH RAILWAYS

IN COLOUR

A Second Glance
1947-1970

**The 1.50pm Ballinamore to Arigna
rattles along the tramway between Ballyduff
and Drumshambo on Tuesday 25th June 1957
hauled by one of the original
Cavan & Leitrim Railway's 4-4-0 tanks,
built for the line in the 1880s.**
Neil Sprinks

To Christopher

Copyright 1995 Tom Ferris

Published by
Midland Publishing Limited
24 The Hollow, Earl Shilton
Leicester, LE9 7NA
England

ISBN 1 85780 019 2

Printed in Hong Kong

Designed by
Midland Publishing Limited
and Stephen Thompson Associates.

Typeset
in 8 on 10 and 9 on 11pt Garamond
and Gill Sans.

Tom Ferris

IRISH RAILWAYS

IN COLOUR

A Second Glance
1947-1970

Midland Publishing
Limited

ACKNOWLEDGEMENTS

A book like this is first and foremost a celebration of the work of the photographers whose pictures are featured in its pages. If a great many individuals had not taken the trouble to use the slow and expensive colour films available in the 1950s and '60s, then its compilation would have been impossible.

Pictures have come from two sources, the portfolios of the individual photographers who took the pictures themselves or from collections made by other persons who have thus saved for posterity the work of photographers who may have passed on.

Individual photographers who have allowed me to use their pictures in this book are Keith Bannister, Dennis Bates, Graham Bell, Bryan Boyle, Keith Christie, Michael Costeloe, J G Dewing, John Edgington, Des FitzGerald, John Spencer Gilks, Denis Grimshaw, A D Hutchinson, M A Jose, John Laird, John Langford, R C Ludgate, David Murray, Walter Mc Grath, Craig Robb, F W Shuttleworth, D A Soggee, Neil Sprinks, R Tourret, Keith Walton, Richard Whitford and Derek Young.

I am grateful to the following organisations and collectors for access to their material. Ron White of Colour Rail has produced many images of Irish railways which have not appeared in his published catalogues; Philip Atkins of the National Railway Museum in York arranged for me to see some slides which are in the care of the NRM, taken by John G Click, who was Bulleid's assistant at Inchicore; Cyril Fry, best known as the doyen of Irish railway modellers, whose work is celebrated in a permanent exhibition, the Fry Model Railway at Malahide Castle in County Dublin, was also active as a photographer. His colour slides are now in the collection of Hassard Stacpoole who has generously given me access to this material. Mike Jose has allowed me to use images taken by the late John Phillips which are in his care. Other pictures have come from the Midland Publishing collection.

I am grateful to Charles Friel and John Langford who read the page proofs and rescued me from a number of errors which had crept into the manuscript. Thanks are due to Des Mc Glynn and Clifton Flewitt for providing or verifying much of the information in Chapter Six and to John Kennedy for doing the same for the pages which feature the 800 class locomotives, on which he is the acknowledged expert. Joe Curran, a son of B L Curran – the last general manager of the County Donegal narrow gauge system, ran an expert eye over the CDR pages and passed them fit for human consumption. The map of the Irish railway system in 1947 was specially produced for this book by Stephen Johnson. It has been extracted from the very thorough database which he has been building for some time. Midland hope to release the fruits of his meticulous research in 1996. *Johnson's Atlas and Gazetteer of the Railways of Ireland*, will we believe, offer the most comprehensive reference and cartographic coverage of the Irish railway system ever published.

Friends and colleagues, too numerous to mention, on both sides of the Irish Sea, have offered much advice and support in the course of producing this volume. My colleagues at Midland Publishing, Chris Salter and Steve Thompson, who have created the distinctive and well received style which our railway books possess, have once again shaped this book and guided it through the seemingly byzantine complexities of the production process.

To all those who have contributed in so many ways may I offer sincere thanks and hope that you will not be disappointed by the finished article.

One of the most surprising developments of the 1950s was the complete modernisation of the West Clare narrow gauge system. Once a byword for unpunctuality and unreliability, the introduction by CIE of diesel railcars and locomotives transformed the line into the most well equipped narrow gauge railway in Ireland. In August 1958, one of the railcars pauses at Ennistimon on a service to Kilkee. Keith Christie

CONTENTS

Title page:
**J19 class 0-6-0 No 610 has just arrived
at Loughrea with a mixed branch train from
Attymon Junction on 14th August 1961.**
J G Dewing

INTRODUCTION

When I set out in 1991, on the path that led to the publication of what became *Irish Railways in Colour: From Steam to Diesel 1955-1967*, there were many imponderables ahead which could have derailed the project at any time. Whilst I was reasonably certain that there was considerable and growing interest in the railways of Ireland, this could not be quantified in any scientific way. I was pursuing a hunch, both as an author and a publisher, which fortuitously proved to be correct, namely that this interest, combined with the lack of material in print on the subject, was sufficient to justify the large print run which a colour book dictates.

An even more fundamental uncertainty lay in the question of whether enough colour material existed from the 1950s and '60s to enable a reasonably comprehensive pictorial record of the railways of Ireland to be provided, in the period which saw the changeover from steam to diesel. As no colour album on the subject had ever been published before, it was possible that the reason that such a book had never appeared was that simply the supply of colour images did not exist in either sufficient quantity or quality. With these thoughts in mind the search for colour pictures began. Starting with a small number of photographers, mostly based in Ireland, the list of potential contributors gradually broadened, largely

because of the assistance given by those who we had approached in the first place. As time went on the net widened and more photographers and photographic sources emerged to assist the project than could have been hoped for in the first place. More than enough colour images were unearthed in the end to produce the book, more or less, in the form we had envisaged.

A few pictures had to be used which were not as good as we might have wished for. These were used to cover a particular class or section of line which would otherwise not have been featured in the book. The forbearance of readers and reviewers was sought in relation to these, and most accepted that there was an imprecise equation involving a balance between the rarity of the subject, the necessity of its inclusion and the quality of the available material. Readers also generously accepted that in a book of vintage colour images, to some extent, the availability of the material, determined the structure of the book and what was or was not included in its content. To a degree, though I think to a lesser extent, I ask you again to accept these caveats, in this sequel.

In that first volume, *Irish Railways in Colour: From Steam to Diesel 1955-1967*, it was felt essential to provide a fairly comprehensive account of the structure and the operators of the Irish railway system in the

period covered by the book. This was due to the fact that so little had been published, at least in Britain, on the subject for so long. Rather than repeat all of this again in this second volume, subtitled *A Second Glance: 1947-1970* – this information is kept to the minimum which readers new to the subject will need to understand what is going on, where the lines are located, who built them and who subsequently came to control them. I have endeavoured to give primacy to the pictures on the self evident premise that one cracking colour image can say more than a thousand words of text, no matter how carefully crafted.

Perhaps the most significant thing to emerge in the wake of the publication of the first volume, was that it encouraged many photographers to get in touch with us to offer material for a possible sequel. This has meant that many more images have been examined for possible inclusion in this book than had been available for the first volume. Yet even though we have gone from not quite a famine to something approaching a feast, and in terms of the number of pages this new volume is around 20% bigger, and contains many more images, we have still, albeit with great reluctance, had to leave out many excellent pictures. If the demand is there, enough material is to hand already to provide the bones of a third volume in the series, before contemplating any further gems which additional research would undoubtedly bring to light.

The original intention was that this sequel would be called *Irish Steam in Colour*. This was to distinguish it from a colour book devoted to Irish diesel and electric traction, which is in preparation. This idea was jettisoned at an early stage for two reasons. To begin with, I realised that I had probably underestimated the very great interest which has grown up in recent years in the diesel locomotives and railcars which had displaced steam from Ireland's railways. In addition to this, because steam traction disappeared so rapidly in the Irish Republic I felt that to ignore the coming of the diesels would have offered an unbalanced view of that system in particular. To have excluded

Left: **Ex-GNR S class 4-4-0 No 171 *Slieve Gullion*** heads the 10.32 Belfast to Portadown goods near Derriaghy on the crisp morning of 8th February 1964. Craig Robb.

the pioneering diesel railcars of the Great Northern and the County Donegal, not to mention CIE's fleet of main line diesel locomotives would have produced a portrait of the Irish railway network in the 1950s and '60s which was potentially misleading and which would have lost one of the most fascinating aspects of the period, the interface between the old and the new, which characterised these years. Therefore, whilst there is a preponderance of steam in this book, the diesels do feature in its pages for good reasons. In addition, in an attempt to provide a more complete picture of the activities of the railway operators in the country, some coverage is included of railway owned tramways and buses, an engrossing subject in its own right and one often ignored. It is my hope that both steam and modern traction enthusiasts will feel satisfied by the coverage given to their particular interests in the chapters that follow, though it is a moot point whether, in the context of Irish railways, the term 'modern traction' is at all appropriate, when applied to diesel railcars dating back to the 1930s and an electric railway opened in the reign of Queen Victoria.

I have tried to cover the broadest possible canvas in the pages which follow. The pictures have been chosen to portray as many types of locomotives and varieties of train workings as could be found. The geographical locations featured range through-out Ireland, north and south. As was the case with *Irish Railways in Colour: From Steam to Diesel 1955-1967*, though to a lesser extent this time round, the availability of material has helped to shape the structure of the book. To give one example, there is a considerable imbalance in the photographic record between colour pictures of CIE steam locomotives in action and those operated by the Ulster Transport Authority. This is simply due to the fact that steam traction lasted much longer in Northern Ireland than it did in the Irish Republic. This also coincided with the wider availability of colour film at more reasonable prices from about 1960 onwards. Despite this, I have tried to represent CIE steam as comprehensively as possible and also to restrain my freely admitted prejudice in favour of anything bearing the initials GNR! If your favourite locomotive or stretch of line is not included it is probably due to the absence of colour material rather than for any other reason and I hope you will share my delight at what has been recorded in colour rather than be disappointed at what has not.

A great many kind letters were received from people on both sides of the Irish Sea, and indeed beyond, as a result of the publication of the first volume. Many of these related to specific pictures or groups of pictures which stirred memories or brought to life long closed lines, for those who never had the chance to experience them when they were still in existence. These letters were the surest way of judging that the book had been worth doing and had given pleasure to a lot of people. For many, the highlights of the book were those wonderful pictures taken by the late Gerry Douglas, of the Great Northern lines in County Cavan, not long before they closed in the late 1950s. I felt it would be difficult to match those in any sequel, but such is the range and quality of the images which have been brought to light since 1992, that I am certain that some of the pictures or sets of pictures in the pages which follow, will have an equal or greater impact, to those memorable images from the first book.

For better or worse, and I hope readers think the former, this book is as good as its pictures. I have been astonished at both the rarity and the quality of some of the pictures which have turned up in the course of the research. Colour pictures of subjects and locations which I could scarcely have hoped to find, have appeared. These range from the earliest colour images of Ireland's railways which I have found so far, dating from the 1940s, to what was probably the last occasion when a steam locomotive was used by a railway operator on official business in these islands. In the photographs throughout the period covered by the book, from 1947 to 1970, I promise you many pleasant surprises and a host of images which will linger long in your memory.

Once again I am indebted to the photographers who took the pictures which make up this book and who are acknowledged separately elsewhere. Both as individuals and collectively they have enabled future generations to relive the variety and interest which the railways of Ireland presented in the years covered by this book. They have allowed us to make this colourful and nostalgic trip back in time. I hope you enjoy the journey, and in the words of the old Irish proverb, 'may the road rise up to meet you'.

Tom Ferris
Shrewsbury, May 1995.

Below: **A pair of CIE General Motors 141 class Bo-Bo diesels, led by B145, are about to leave Dublin's Heuston, formerly Kingsbridge station with the 8.45am express for Cork, on 12th April 1969.** Craig Robb.

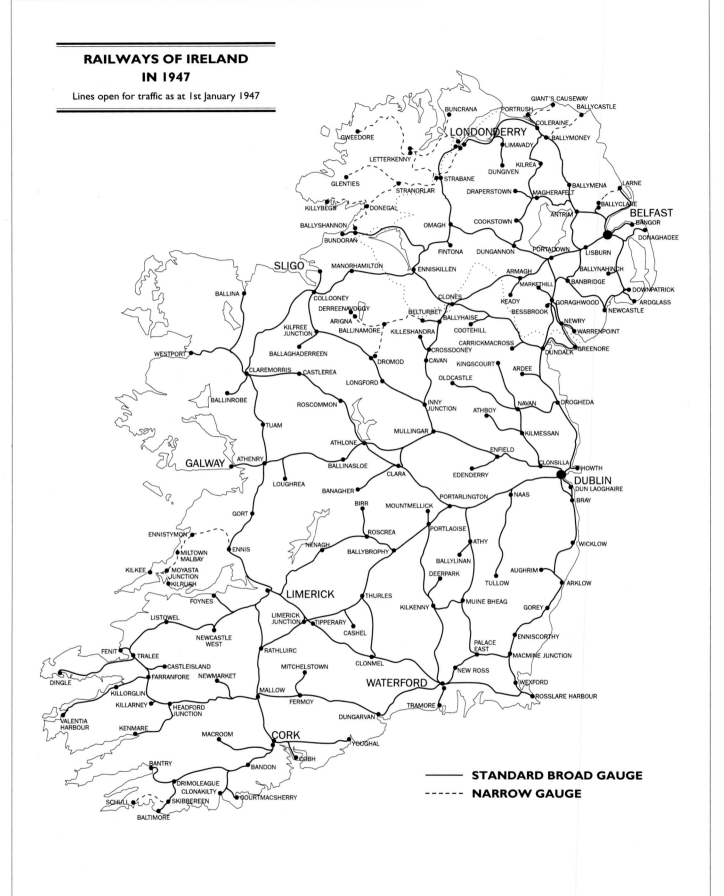

RAILWAYS OF IRELAND IN 1947

Lines open for traffic as at 1st January 1947

STANDARD BROAD GAUGE
NARROW GAUGE

CIE

FROM STEAM TO DIESEL

The railways of the Irish Free State, which became the Republic of Ireland in 1948, had been run by the Great Southern Railways from 1925 to 1945. The GSR had been formed through the state sponsored grouping of those railways wholly located within the Free State. In 1945, the GSR and the Dublin United Transport Company, which provided bus and tram services in Ireland's capital, were amalgamated to form Coras Iompair Eireann, which was given a monopoly of road and rail transport in the southern part of Ireland. Those railways like the Great Northern and the Sligo, Leitrim & Northern Counties which entered Northern Ireland were unaffected by the formation of the GSR and CIE.

CIE inherited over 2,500 track miles which were almost exclusively worked by the company's fleet of nearly 600 steam locomotives which was made up of over 100 different classes. There had been very little development of the steam fleet during the GSR years. Very few new locomotives were constructed and the steam stock which CIE took over was very little changed from that which had come to the GSR in 1925 from the independent Irish companies.

The 1930s were bleak years in the Irish Free State, with the country's leader Eamon de Valera conducting a futile economic war with Britain. There was little money to invest in the country's railways which the motley CIE steam fleet reflected.

It is not surprising that the company resorted to dieselisation as soon as funds were available in the 1950s. The aged and diverse steam locomotives, which were a delight for the railway enthusiast, must have been a nightmare for those who had to try and maintain any sort of service with them. This, coupled with the problem of getting a reliable supply of coal in the post war years, hastened the rapid replacement of steam, as soon as the funding could be obtained and utilised to purchase diesel railcars and locomotives.

In this chapter we are concentrating on the 5ft 3in gauge lines of CIE – the 3ft narrow gauge operations of the company are dealt with in Chapter Five.

Above: **The GSR may have had to run Ireland's railways in a period of economic sterility but the company will forever be associated with the three magnificent 800 class locomotives built at Inchicore in 1939-40 and given names from the mists of Celtic antiquity. Comparable in size to the 'Kings' of the Great Western** Railway and the 'Royal Scots' of the London Midland & Scottish Railway, these magnificent machines were among the largest 4-6-0s to be seen anywhere in Europe and though wartime conditions and lack of a reliable coal supply after the war deprived them of the opportunity to display their full potential, they are by some way the largest and most impressive steam locomotives ever to grace Ireland's railways. Their size and weight restricted them to the Dublin to Cork main line. Here No 801 *Macha* is being prepared to work a service to Dublin at Cork's Glanmire Road shed in July 1947. A D Hutchinson

THE 800s

Officially designated the B1a class, but more commonly referred to as the 800s, it has been mistakenly assumed by many, including the author, it must be said, that the three locomotives, *Meadhbh*, *Macha* and *Tailte*, were named after ancient Celtic Queens. In fact they are named after deities in the pre-Christian Celtic pantheon. This confusion has probably arisen through there being both a deity and a famous warrior Queen, called Meave, the latter celebrated in the Tain, that great ancient epic of Celtic culture, comparable to the Iliad and Beowulf.

Top left: **This rear three-quarter view of No 801, taken in July 1947, shows her gold lining, green livery and the CIE logo on her tender to, good effect.** A D Hutchinson

Centre left: **No 800, *Meadhbh*, shunts an extra carriage onto a train at Dublin's Kingsbridge station on a damp and dreary, or as it is known in Ireland, a soft day, in the mid-1950s.** John Click / courtesy National Railway Museum

Bottom: **This undated view of No 802 *Tailte*, at Glanmire Road shed in Cork was taken sometime in the late 1950s. No 802 was the first of the trio to be withdrawn and may have already been in store awaiting its fate when this picture was taken.** John Click / courtesy National Railway Museum

THE OTHER 4-6-0s

Above left: **E A Watson, the designer of the 400 class, came to Inchicore from the GWR at Swindon in 1914 determined to introduce a 4-cylindered express engine based on GWR practice. These, the only 4-cylinder engines ever to run in Ireland, proved to be a disappointment. Though clearly based on Churchward's 'Star' class engines on the GWR, as** built they were unsuccessful and the majority were rebuilt as 2-cylinder machines. Three unrebuilt locomotives were scrapped in 1929-30, but the remainder gave good service to the GSR and CIE. No 402 was at Killarney on 7th September 1954, on an up working. R Tourret

Below: **400 class No 407 which was rebuilt by the GSR as late as 1937, is seen after arrival at Portarlington on the main line to Cork, with a test train from Inchicore in September 1958.**
Cyril Fry / H Stacpoole collection

Above right: **The other class of 4-6-0 tender engine to run in Ireland on the broad gauge was the 500 class which was built at Inchicore between 1924 and 1926 to the design of J R Bazin. Though not as heavy or as powerful as the 800s, they had a reputation as strong reliable machines. This, the only colour picture of the class I have ever seen, shows No 502 leaving Kingsbridge station in Dublin with an express for Cork on 7th July 1948.**
A D Hutchinson

Top: **An interesting contrast between the 400 and 800 class 4-6-0s is provided in this picture of No 800 *Maedhbh* out of service but earmarked for preservation, and No 401 which was still at work, when this picture was taken on 24th May 1960, at Thurles.** J G Dewing

Above: **Near the end of its days No 401 brings a long train of sugar beet empties into Mallow station from the nearby sugar factory on 3rd November 1960.** John Langford

INCHICORE

Right: **Ireland's largest railway works and the citadel in turn of Great Southern & Western Railway, GSR and CIE steam, was situated a short distance out of Kingsbridge station in Dublin. A train of CIE railcars on their way to Kingsbridge on 7th October 1961, pass the ornate castellated side of the works which fronted the Cork main line. Inchicore's similarly and uniquely castellated signal box can be glimpsed above the second coach.**
Cyril Fry / H Stacpoole collection

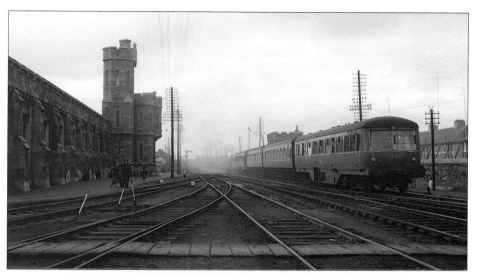

Centre: **For many years a special was run from Kingsbridge to Inchicore for the benefit of those who worked there. One of Ivatt's F6 2-4-2 tanks dating from the 1890s departs towards Kingsbridge with such a working consisting of one 6-wheeled coach of considerable vintage, on 6th September 1954.** R Tourret

Bottom: **Richard Maunsell produced only one design for the GS&WR in his short spell in charge at Inchicore before he left for the South Eastern & Chatham Railway – a 0-4-2 saddle tank. Built in 1914, the year after its designer's departure, for decades it was the shunter at the works. To my knowledge it was never given a number but it had a name, *Sambo*. Maunsell's influence on the railways of his native land was exercised much more strongly by a locomotive design he produced for the SECR, than by anything he did when he was in charge at Inchicore.** John Phillips

THE WOOLWICH MOGULS

R E L Maunsell, a native of Dublin, was the works manager at Inchicore for a number of years before his relatively short spell as locomotive superintendent of the GS&WR from 1911 to 1913. In that year he moved to a similar position with the South Eastern & Chatham Railway. His first new design for the SECR was a taper boilered, outside cylindered, mixed-traffic 2-6-0 introduced in 1917. This class and a subsequent variant with slightly larger driving wheels was very successful and a number lasted until the end of steam on the Southern Region of British Railways in the late 1960s. In order to maintain employment after the war, in 1920 the government arranged for no less than 100 Maunsell Moguls to be constructed by former munitions workers at Woolwich Arsenal in south east London. Spotting a bargain, the Midland Great Western Railway bought 12 of these engines in kit form in 1924, just before the Irish grouping. The GSR acquired a further 15 sets of parts in the next two years though only 26 of these kits ever became working locomotives. The Woolwich Moguls, as the class was commonly called, gave as good a service to the GSR and CIE as their counterparts did in England to the Southern Railway and the Southern Region of BR, lasting like their English counterparts, until the end of steam operations on CIE.

Top: **A grimy Mogul No 385 is seen at Amiens Street shed in Dublin.** David Murray

Left: **Maunsell Moguls ran on both sides of the Irish Sea. British Railways N class Mogul No 31412, one of the early engines built for the SECR in 1917 is seen leaving Farnborough North in Surrey on 12th October 1963.** J G Dewing

Above: **The Woolwich Moguls were for many years associated with the former MGWR lines to the west of Ireland. On 16th August 1953 No 378 is seen at the former MGWR shed at** the Broadstone in Dublin. It is of interest to compare the Maunsell Moguls which ran on both sides of the Irish Sea. Tractive effort, boiler pressure and cylinder dimensions of the two were identical, although the Irish engines were slightly heavier. The most obvious difference was the smoke deflectors later carried by the British locomotives. R Tourret

Above: **On 8th July 1960 No 372 has just arrived on shed at the Broadstone having been on pilot duties at the goods yards at the North Wall that day.** David Murray

Bottom: **On 15th March 1959 green liveried Mogul No 378 is on shed at the Broadstone. The former MGWR shed closed in 1961.** John Langford

Left: CIE and the companies before it, relied heavily on 4-4-0s for passenger services, many surviving into our period. D17 class No 18 was at Athenry in March 1956. This class was designed by J A F Aspinall who was in charge at Inchicore between 1883 and 1886. He later moved to England where he gained a considerable reputation and a knighthood, for his work on the Lancashire & Yorkshire Railway.

Centre left: **D17 No 4, built in 1888, shunts at Tralee in July 1956.**

Below: **D11 Class 4-4-0 No 301 was built to Coey's design in 1900. It was rebuilt in 1931 with a superheated boiler. The locomotive is framed by the two splendid sets of lower quadrant signals at the ends of the platforms at Limerick station, in J G Dewing's photograph, which was taken on 15th March 1961.**

Opposite page top: **Another Aspinall design became the GSR's D14 class. No 89 was built in 1886, and was reboiled at least twice. It is seen here at Bray on 1st June 1957.** J G Dewing

Opposite page bottom: **Coey's D2 class was built between 1904 and 1906. No 329, reboiled in 1929 and 1932, is seen in its final form at Kingsbridge in July 1956.**

Unattributed photographs on this page are by the late J A Whaley / Colour Rail

THE J15s

By far the most numerous class of steam locomotives in Irish railway history was the 101 class of the GS&WR, the J15s of the GSR and CIE. Introduced by Alexander McDonnell in the 1860s, these sturdy 0-6-0s were the work horses of the railways of the south of Ireland for many decades.

Top: **Like many of the class, No 154, built by Beyer Peacock in 1868, was rebuilt, in this case in 1941, with a superheated boiler. The locomotive was recorded at Birr, the terminus of a branch from Roscrea on the Ballybrophy to Limerick line, on Tuesday 18th August 1959. The train is the 3.45pm Birr to Roscrea service. The photographer recalls that the branch train was mixed, conveying goods wagons as well as passenger coaches. A generous 35 minutes were allowed to cover the 11 mile long line.** John Langford

Above: **No 162 was built in 1871. Pictured shunting at Limerick on 15th March 1961, she retains a round topped saturated boiler and an old fashioned type of tender with springs on the outside. In general the locomotive looks much as she would have done when built some 90 years before.** J G Dewing

Above: **Two J15s have been preserved and are in the care of the Railway Preservation Society of Ireland. One of these locomotives, No 184, was turned out in lined green in 1955 and is seen here hauling a transfer freight from the North Wall at Islandbridge Junction, just outside Kings-bridge, on 24th May 1960.** J G Dewing

Below: **The J15s were used all over the CIE system. No 183, by dint of its superheated boiler and larger, more modern tender looking rather differ-ent from its sister No 184 in the above picture, was recorded at Athlone on the former MGWR line to the west, in the early 1960s.** Colour Rail

OTHER 0-6-0s

Virtually every Irish railway company operated 0-6-0 tender engines. Though usually associated with goods traffic, the various types of 0-6-0 were also frequently used on passenger trains. The last new 0-6-0s to enter service in Ireland were delivered to the Great Northern as late as 1948. Fifteen new 0-6-0s were built by the GSR between 1929 and 1934. Numbered in the 700 series, the two variants of the design were classified J15a and J15b. In theory improved versions of the J15s, in fact they seem to have been less well thought of than the venerable design they were supposed to have bettered. Surprisingly the J15as were built with saturated boilers though the J15bs had the Z class superheated boiler which was fitted to many of the J15s as they were rebuilt.

Top: **The year before it was withdrawn, J15a No 704 was shunting in the former Midland goods yard at the North Wall in Dublin on 21st March 1959.** W P de Beer / Colour Rail

Centre left: **The J9 class was introduced by Coey in 1903 and a further batch was built in 1912. No 252 has just been turned at Youghal in this September 1962 view.** John Edgington

Bottom left: **J9 No 249 poses outside the shed at Waterford.** Graham Bell

Bottom right: **The J4 class, built in 1913/14 was another Coey 0-6-0 design for the GS&WR. No 262 lies out of use at Inchicore in the early 1960s. Alongside it is J15 No 198. The white spot on the J15's tender indicates that it had been converted to oil burning during the period of coal shortages after the Second World War. Though it had long reverted to coal firing its tender must not have seen a paint brush in the intervening years.** Graham Bell

THE TURF BURNER

Of the many steam locomotives built at Inchicore over the years, the last was probably the most unusual. Maunsell, who went from Inchicore to the SECR, eventually became the Chief Mechanical Engineer of the Southern Railway, a post he held until 1937 when he was succeeded by O V S Bulleid. Following the nationalisation of the railways of Britain in 1948 Bulleid moved to Ireland to become the CME of CIE. His last design for his former employers was the controversial 'Leader' class, an experimental tank engine on 6-wheel bogies with a cab at each end, a third cab in the centre for the fireman and incorporating a host of untried features. After considerable expenditure the design was abandoned. Unbowed by this spectacular failure Bulleid brought the 'Leader' concept with him to Ireland where he tried to apply its basic principles to Irish conditions. One problem which had bedevilled CIE steam operations after the war was a shortage of decent coal, some locomotives being converted to oil burning to cope with this. Bulleid's original mind turned to the one fuel which Ireland had in large quantities, turf, or peat as it is known outside Ireland. He built a steam locomotive, based on the ideas which had already been proved defective in England, with the difference that it was to burn turf. In Bulleid's distinctive system of numbering where a letter denoted the number of coupled axles, it was known as CC1, but it was more commonly referred to as 'The Turf Burner'. It emerged from Inchicore in 1957 and ran some trials in 1957/58. 'The Turf Burner' never entered revenue earning service and with Bulleid's retirement in 1958 no further development of the locomotive was carried out. It lingered at Inchicore forlorn and out of use until scrapped in 1965.

Top: **As a test bed for some of the ideas which were to be incorporated in CC1, Bulleid converted K3 Class 2-6-0 No 356 to burn turf in 1952. Looking rather sorry for itself, the much abused K3 was photographed at Inchicore on 16th August 1953.** R Tourret

Centre: **Proudly taking its place outside the running shed at Inchicore not long after it was built in 1957, the unconventional appearance of 'The Turf Burner', which is in steam on this occasion, can be appreciated by comparison with the other locomotives in the picture.** John Click / courtesy National Railway Museum

Bottom: **This rare colour picture of 'The Turf Burner' on a test train was taken by John Click who worked with Bulleid on the project, at Portarlington, in mid-1958. The evidence that the machine is working is the steam or smoke which partly obscures the tall tree to its left.** Courtesy National Railway Museum

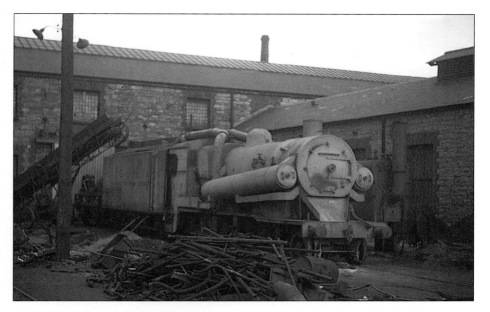

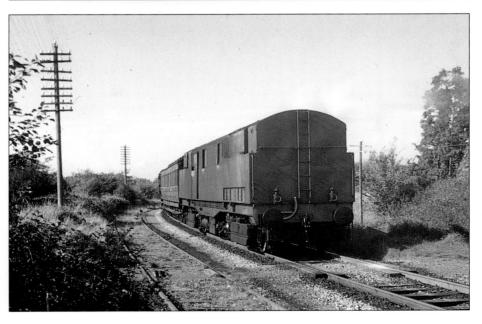

D&SER SCENES

Having looked at some of the significant steam locomotive types to be found on the CIE system in the 1950s we will commence a leisurely rail tour around the network, beginning with some scenes from the lines of the former Dublin & South Eastern Railway.

Top: **Ireland's first railway was from Dublin to Kingstown, known today as Dun Laoghaire. At** the time it was built in the 1830s, Dublin was the second city after London in the British Empire. The importance of getting mail quickly via the short sea route from Kingstown to Holyhead was the making of both ports and encouraged the promotion of the lines which linked them to their capitals. This view, taken on 9th July 1960, shows the short branch line onto the Carlisle Pier where the steamers berthed. It was lifted when the main line was electrified in the 1980s. The ships have changed to roll-on roll-off car ferries but the buildings are largely the same today. J G Dewing

Above: **The D&SER station at Westland Row was connected to the GNR terminus at Amiens Street on the other side of the River Liffey by the City of Dublin Junction Railway which was opened in 1891. Today the line is electrified and carries the frequent DART (Dublin Area Rapid Transit) services which run from Bray to Howth. In the diesel era these suburban services were operated mostly by C class diesels, one of which, impersonating a steam locomotive, as they often did, is seen on the viaducts of the former C&DJR in the early 1960s.** Graham Bell

BRAY HEAD

One of the most scenic stretches of railway in Ireland is that between Bray and Greystones on the route from Dublin to Wicklow and Rosslare. The section of line between Bray and Wicklow was opened in 1855 by the Dublin & Wicklow Railway. The railway tunnels through Bray Head and then clings to a ledge carved along the cliff face. Coastal erosion has always been a problem since the line was built. Of the four tunnels on this stretch, the longest was built in 1917 when the railway was moved some yards inland to try and overcome the erosion problem. In these views taken by A D Hutchinson in July 1950, both the spectacular setting of the line and the problems it has posed can be appreciated.

Top: **C2 class 4-4-2T No 456, built by Beyer Peacock in 1924 for the D&SER, brings a train heading south to Wicklow, out of one of the tunnels.**

Right: **The full spectacle of this stretch is captured in this view of a Wicklow bound train. From this perspective one can appreciate the difficulties the builders of the line must have encountered as well as those of the staff who have had to maintain it over the years.**

Above: **The former D&SER main line closely follows the coast as far as Wicklow. From there it turns inland and runs down the beautiful and wooded Vale of Avoca to Woodenbridge, which was the junction for the branch to Shillelagh until its closure in 1944. In July 1950, whilst working a northbound goods an ex-D&SER 0-6-0 shunts at Woodenbridge with the River Avoca in the background .**
A D Hutchinson

Centre: **The last locomotive ordered by the D&SER was their No 35, a 4-4-2T built by Beyer Peacock in 1924. This became No 457 under the GSR and CIE. Withdrawn in 1959, though rusted and awaiting its date with the cutting torch, the handsome lines of the machine can still be appreciated in Keith Bannister's picture.**

Bottom: **The only surviving D&SER locomotive is No 461, which also has the distinction of being the only inside cylindered Mogul still in existence in the British Isles. The locomotive, one of two such machines delivered by Beyer Peacock in 1922, was preserved by CIE when it was withdrawn from service. It is now in the care of the Railway Preservation Society of Ireland and has been used regularly on rail tours around the county. In June 1961, before it was preserved, it was recorded when working a special train for railway enthusiasts at Kilkenny.** John Edgington

DUBLIN'S LOST RAILWAY

Of all the lines abandoned in Ireland in the 1950s and '60s, perhaps none has caused so much heart searching as the closure, at the end of 1958, of the former D&SER route from Bray to Harcourt Street station in Dublin. On the face of it, and in keeping with the prevailing anti-railway rhetoric of the time, it duplicated the coastal line from Bray to Dublin, so it had to go. But the Harcourt Street line served communities like Dundrum, Stillorgan and Foxrock which were no longer country villages but suburbs of the expanding city. In any sensible environment, their railway would have been electrified and the services expanded. In Ireland it was closed. Today much of the trackbed and many of the structures still exist and from the outside Harcourt Street station looks much the same as the day it closed. One argument in favour of the line closing was that the terminus was too far from the centre of the city, but there is room to build a gentle ramp down from its platform which would give today's breed of 'Supertrams' access to the streets, along which a short glide would take them to the corner of Saint Stephen's Green and Grafton Street, in the very heart of Dublin. As an alternative the trams could take to the streets where the line crossed the Grand Canal. Our pictures of the line in its last days in December 1958 were taken by Michael Costeloe

Top and centre right: **The 1.25pm railcar for Bray waits at Harcourt Street's platform on 30th December 1958. The three lines converged onto a turntable at the far end of the train shed.**

Bottom: **On 13th December 1958, the 3.25pm train for Bray pauses at Ranelagh, the first station out of Harcourt Street.**

WEXFORD

Top left: **One of the last bastions of steam passenger workings on CIE was in County Wexford. On 9th June 1962, the 8.15am local passenger working from Rosslare Harbour passes along the quays at Wexford on its way to the town's main station.** John Langford

Top right: **A J15 heads a permanent way train along the quay on 4th April 1961.**
Cyril Fry / H Stacpoole collection

Centre left: **J15 No 187 leaves the now closed Wexford South station with a train for Rosslare in April 1961.**
Cyril Fry / H Stacpoole collection.

Below: **North of Wexford, on the route to Dublin, was Macmine Junction from where a line ran to Waterford via New Ross. We begin our exploration of this line at Macmine Junction. The train in the picture is the 7.25am Dublin Westland Row to Rosslare Harbour, formed of an ex-Great Northern BUT railcar set headed by No c 904 n. The next vehicle to this, still in GNR blue and cream, is followed by a carriage in the then new CIE black and orange livery, quite a kaleidoscope all in all! The date was 9th June 1962.** John Langford

PALACE EAST

Top right: On the line from Wexford to Waterford via Macmine Junction and New Ross there was a junction at a remote spot called Palace East. From here a line ran north to Bagenalstown on the route used by today's Dublin to Waterford expresses. Though this line lost its passenger services as long ago as 1931 it remained open for freight, especially the seasonal sugar beet traffic, until the 1960s. On 17th December 1959, J9 class 0-6-0 No 354, paired with an old tender with outside springs, approaches Palace East with the 10.40am passenger train from Waterford to Wexford. The other single line to the right of the engine is the branch to Bagenalstown. John Langford

Centre right: On the same day J15 No 198 has arrived in the branch platform at Palace East with a beet special from the Bagenalstown line. John Langford

Below: **Lack of siding space at Palace East and the almost simultaneous arrival of two passenger trains and the beet special led to the third train in this sequence, the 10.00am passenger from Wexford to Waterford, being put into the head-shunt. Part of the beet train, which had to be divided to allow the passenger train to get there in the first place, can be seen in the foreground, beyond this the tall D&SER signal is off for the arrival of the train from Waterford.** John Langford

NEW ROSS
AND WATERFORD

Top: **The now preserved J15 No 186 is seen working the 10.00am passenger train from Wexford to Waterford at New Ross on 17th December 1959.** John Langford

Above: **Steam could be found at Waterford on seasonal beet workings, freight and local passenger services until the early 1960s. Here J15 No 134, in poor external condition, shunts in the goods yard alongside the River Suir to the west of Waterford station on 17th December 1959.** John Langford

MALLOW

From Waterford we move west to explore some railways of County Cork. We begin with contrasting views taken at Mallow, on the Dublin to Cork main line, in the 1950s.

Top: **A fleet of Metropolitan Vickers diesels quickly banished steam from CIE's main line passenger trains. One of these A class diesels arrives at Mallow on 10th June 1958 with CIE's Radio Train. This is en route from Dublin to Killarney and provided music and a commentary on the passing scenery for passengers.** Midland Publishing collection

Above: **On 27th June 1959, Metropolitan Vickers diesel A17 arrives at Mallow with a boat train from Cork to Rosslare, which traversed the now closed line from Mallow, through Dungarvan to Waterford.** Michael Costeloe

GLANMIRE ROAD

Left: **Cork's main station was at Glanmire Road, where the services from Dublin terminated. A graceful curving train shed, seen behind the trains in the picture, spanned the main line tracks, which, immediately beyond the station, plunged into a tunnel. At the eastern end of the station were the bays which were used by trains for the branches to Cobh and Youghal. Today Glanmire Road is the only station serving Cork City. J15 No 170 prepares to depart with the 2.30pm to Youghal on 9th July 1960.** Colour Rail

Centre: **J15 No 193 seen at Glanmire Road on Saint Patrick's Day, 17th March 1962, has been specially spruced up to work a rail tour on the east Cork branches. This locomotive was built in 1898 by the GS&WR. It was rebuilt with a superheated boiler in 1948 by CIE and lasted until 1963.** J G Dewing

Bottom: **B4 class 4-6-0 tank No 468 built in 1910 for the Cork, Bandon & South Coast Railway by Beyer Peacock, shunts empty coaching stock at Glanmire Road on 26th May 1960.** J G Dewing

EAST CORK BRANCHES

The lines to Cobh and Yougal were opened by the independent Cork & Yougal Railway between 1859 and 1862. The C&Y was absorbed by the GS&WR shortly afterwards in 1866.

Top: **Cobh or Queenstown as it was formerly known, was for many years a port of call for trans-Atlantic steamers. In 1912 the ill-fated *Titanic* paused here before sailing off to her rendezvous with history. The branch has always had a healthy local traffic to and from Cork. On a Sunday afternoon in July 1947, J15 No 146 heads a train of 6-wheelers out of Cobh bound for the city. Most of the carriages** are still in the GSR's claret or crimson livery. A D Hutchinson

Above: **The line to Youghal left the Cobh route at Cobh Junction heading due east to reach its destination. J4 0-6-0 No 262 has just arrived at Youghal with a train from Cork in September 1962.** John Edgington

CORK SHEDS

Top: **Glanmire Road shed was situated east of the passenger station. Steam locomotives still dominate on 29th August 1958.** Colour Rail

Centre left: **J30 0-6-0T No 90, dating from 1875, and C class diesel No C231 built in 1957, seen together on shed at Glanmire Road on 17th March 1961 are both among the sadly few 5ft 3in gauge Irish locomotives which have been preserved.** J G Dewing

Bottom: **Cork's other main depot was at Rock-savage serving the former CB&SCR's station at Albert Quay. In August 1953, one of the Bandon 4-6-0 tanks, No 463 is on view.** R Tourret

CORK CITY RAILWAYS

Opposite page top: **The GS&WR system at Glanmire Road and that of the CB&SCR at Albert Quay were joined by a tramway through the streets of the city, grandly known as the Cork City Railways. J11 class 0-6-0 tank No 207, designed by Ivatt and dating from 1887, heads a transfer freight along this line on 18th August 1953 preceded by a man with the statutory red flag.** R Tourret

Opposite page bottom: **Passenger trains did not normally operate on the line through the streets. An exception to this was a rail tour organised by the Irish Railway Record Society in March 1961 to mark the closure of the CB&SCR system in west Cork. Hauled by one of the Bandon tanks No 464, the special gingerly heads towards Albert Quay.**
John Phillips

ALBERT QUAY

Left: **Steam locomotives were still to be found at Albert Quay, the city terminus of the erstwhile Cork, Bandon & South Coast Railway, virtually up to the closure of the system despite the early introduction of the diesel railcars and locomotives on the lines to west Cork. B4 class 4-6-0T No 468, built in 1910 for the CB&SCR, was shunting beside the station's distinctive elevated signal box on 20th August 1960.** Cyril Fry / H Stacpoole collection

Left: **No 552 was one of the ex-MGWR J26 0-6-0Ts, some of which ended their days on the lines in west Cork. It too was seen at Albert Quay on 20th August 1960.**
Cyril Fry / H Stacpoole collection

Below: **Diesel traction in the form of railcars and latterly C class diesel locomotives, was introduced to the former CB&SCR system from 1954 onwards. On 5th September 1959 a train for Bantry led by railcar No 2625 awaits the appointed hour at Albert Quay.**
Michael Costeloe

DIESELS IN WEST CORK

Above: **C 202, in original silver livery, pauses at Ballinhassig with empty wagons for the sugar beet traffic which will be left for loading at various points along the former CB&SC system.** John Langford

Right: **A contrast between the two liveries of the early diesel era on CIE at Bandon station on 3rd November 1960. C 230, on an up goods, is in the new green livery whilst C 202 in the background carries the earlier silver livery. C 202 is working a down train of empty sugar beet wagons. This traffic brought much activity to these lines in the Autumn. Special trains to convey the beet to the sugar factories ran from October to January. In Ireland some beet traffic, between Wellington Bridge in south Wexford and the factory at Mallow is still carried by rail, in contrast to Britain where the traffic has long been abdicated to the roads.** John Langford

Above left: **J26 No 552, built in 1891 by Kitsons for the MGWR, prepares to leave Courtmacsherry on 16th August 1954 with a return excursion to Cork.** Walter McGrath

Above right: **This is the view from the footplate of a J26 as it heads along the tramway near Timoleague.** John Phillips

TIMOLEAGUE & COURTMACSHERRY

This minor railway, which joined the Clonakilty branch of the CB&SCR system at Ballinascarthy, was very popular among railway enthusiasts. Opened in 1891, for part of its length it was that rarity, a broad gauge roadside tramway. Excursionists were conveyed to the sea at Courtmacsherry long after the regular passenger service ended and the line was also used to carry sugar beet traffic until its closure in 1960.

Above centre: **The summertime seaside excursions to Courtmacsherry were dieselised from about 1958 onwards. In the last year in which they ran, a C class looks somehow out of place on the roadside tramway on 31st July 1960.** Cyril Fry / H Stacpoole collection

Left: **J26 No 552, given the name *Robin* by the MGWR, hauls a beet special along the tramway in November 1960.** John Phillips

Top right: **0-6-0T No 552 was a regular performer on the T&C section from around 1954 until the closure of the line: here she is in charge of a train of wagons being loaded with sugar beet at Timoleague in the Autumn of 1960. In the background are the imposing ruins of Timoleague Abbey, a Franciscan foundation dating from the 15th century.** John Phillips

Centre left: **At Ballinascarthy No 552 performs some animated shunting before heading off down the branch with a train of empty beet wagons.** John Langford

Centre right: **The tank engine working on the branch was stabled overnight at Courtmacsherry. On 4th November 1960 No 552 is being coaled from an adjacent wagon at the end of the platform.** John Langford

Bottom: **The lifting train – a sight that was all too common in Ireland as in Britain in the 1960s. Here Bandon tank No 463 was acting as an accomplice to the destruction of its own line when seen near Bantry in June 1962.** John Phillips

RAILWAYS IN KERRY

County Kerry was served by two lines which converged on Tralee. One, running south west from Limerick, served the north of the county. The other, which is still extant, headed west from Mallow on the Dublin to Cork line. Several branches struck off this route to serve locations such as Newmarket, Kenmare, Valentia and Fenit. We shall deal with the Tralee & Dingle narrow gauge line in County Kerry later, in Chapter 5.

Opposite page top: **The branch from Headford Junction to Kenmare was opened in 1893. It was a product of the Light Railways (Ireland) Act of 1889 which encouraged the building of lines such as this to assist the economic development of remote parts of the country. This branch lasted until 1959. Trains on it were normally mixed and steam locomotives were found hauling these right up to its closure. In August 1957 J15 No 193 is about to leave Kenmare with a return working to Headford Junction.** Colour Rail

Opposite page bottom: **Another of the ubiquitous J15s, No 133, shunts in the goods yard at Kenmare on 11th June 1958.**
Midland Publishing collection

Top right: **Killarney is famed throughout the world for its spectacular lake and mountain scenery. Because the line from Mallow to Tralee was built by two separate companies, which met at Killarney, the town's station is a terminus. Westbound trains have to reverse out of the station to proceed to Tralee, those bound for Mallow have to back into the station. C201 is at the head of a train from Tralee to Dublin on 26th June 1959.**
Michael Costeloe

Centre right: **Railcars Nos 2606 and 2613 catch the evening sun at Tralee on 25th June 1959.**
Michael Costeloe

Bottom right: **The 8 mile long branch from Tralee to Fenit was opened in 1887. The line terminated on the pier at Fenit. Freight and regular Sunday excursion trains in summer persisted into the 1970s. J26 0-6-0T No 559 was shunting at Fenit on 27th April 1960.**
Des FitzGerald

CROSS COUNTRY LINES

Centre left: **A train from Limerick to Waterford with J15 No 191 in charge, pauses at Clonmel on 4th July 1958. This cross country route is still open though the service on it is sparse.** Colour Rail

Top: **The other line which served Clonmel is now closed. This ran north to join the Cork main line at Thurles. On 21st March 1960 J15 No 138 shunts the goods from Thurles at Clonmel goods.** J G Dewing

Bottom left: **One of the most celebrated railway locations in Ireland is Limerick Junction. Situated in County Tipperary, over 20 miles from Limerick City, it was opened in 1848 to provide a connection between the GS&WR Dublin to Cork main line and the cross country route of the Waterford, Limerick & Western which crossed the GS&WR line at right angles.** John Edgington

Bottom right: **The station at the junction had one long island platform with bays at either end. From its opening until the track layout was modified in 1967, all main line trains had to reverse over a scissors crossover which divided the long platform in two. In John Edgington's 1964 picture, the IRRS special sits at the part of the island platform used by Dublin to Cork trains, having reversed over the crossover to get there. The Sulzer diesel is standing on the up main line and the track to its right is the down main line.**

Right: **VS class No 207 *Boyne* approaches Portadown with the 2.30pm semi-fast from Dublin on 16th July 1949. The VS class, the ultimate development of the Great Northern 4-4-0, consisted of five locomotives built by Beyer Peacock and delivered only the previous year. These were not only the GNR's last new express passenger engines but probably the last 4-4-0s built anywhere in the world.**
A D Hutchinson.

Bottom: **The VS class of 1948 can be seen as a simple expansion version of the 3-cylinder V class 'Compounds' introduced in 1932. These were the GNR's top link express engines until the arrival of the new 4-4-0s in 1948. With the V class a policy of naming locomotives was resumed, the five 'Compounds' being named after birds of prey. No 83 *Eagle*, entering Portadown on 8th July 1948 with the midday Belfast to Dublin train, retains her original boiler. The class was equipped with new boilers and Belpaire fireboxes of the type fitted to the VS class at this period, *Eagle* getting her's in 1949.** A D Hutchinson

THE 'ENTERPRISE'

Left: **In August 1947 a new non-stop express between Belfast and Dublin was introduced with customs examinations taking place at either terminus. The name of this new train is still perpetuated on the top expresses on the route to this day. On 21st June 1950 VS class 4-4-0 No 208 *Lagan* approaches Portadown with the evening 'Enterprise' bound for Belfast.** A D Hutchinson

Above: **At first there was only one non-stop 'Enterprise' working which left Belfast at 10.30am and returned from Dublin at 5.30pm. However, such was the popularity of the new service that a second train was put on in 1948. S class 4-4-0 No 170 *Errigal* is seen at Knock Bridge, south of Portadown, with the afternoon Belfast to Dublin train on 15th July 1949.** A D Hutchinson

On pages 52 and 53 we have been able to reproduce some of the publicity material which the GNR produced to promote the new 'Enterprise' service. Our thanks are due to Mr A D Hutchinson for putting this material at our disposal.

Above: **Beginning on 2nd October 1950 the morning 'Enterprise' from Belfast was extended through to Cork with an arrival in the southern city at 5.15pm. The northbound working of the Cork-Dublin-Belfast 'Enterprise' is seen here on 26th June 1951 approaching Portadown headed by VS class No 207 *Boyne*. The train is composed of the CIE set used on the service though it has been strengthened by the addition of a GNR coach at its tail. The working of the 'Enterprise' through to Cork ended in 1953.**
A D Hutchinson

Right: **In May 1955 VS class 4-4-0 No 209 *Foyle* brings a down afternoon working of the 'Enterprise' past the GNR's Dundalk Works.**
Michael Costeloe

53

GREAT NORTHERN LOCOMOTIVES

The story of GNR locomotive design over the years is one of continuity rather than radical change. On the face of it the company perpetuated up to the 1940s principles established in the Victorian era with 4-4-0s for passenger services and 0-6-0s for freight. At first glance it might seem backward looking to continue to build locomotives of these wheel arrangements at the time when, across the Irish Sea, Pacifics were being constructed for express duties and 8-coupled locomotives were often seen on goods work. To take this view is to misunderstand fundamentally conditions in Ireland where the much smaller population and general lack of mineral traffic and heavy industry created a good deal less business for the railways than that which pertained in Britain. The basic GNR 4-4-0 and 0-6-0 types were developed and improved over the years notably by the use of superheated boilers on many machines as they became due for rebuilding. They were more than a match for the traffic on offer and not quaint relics from an earlier era. Our brief survey begins with some of the classes of 4-4-0s built from the 1890s up to the 1940s.

GREAT NORTHERN 4-4-0s

Top: **The PP class dated from the 1890s. No 75 seen here at the GNR shed at Adelaide in Belfast on September 4th 1954, was built by Beyer Peacock in 1898. This engine was rebuilt with a superheated boiler in 1931 becoming a PPs in the process.** R Tourret

Centre: **The Q class first appeared in 1899 to the design of Charles Clifford. No 135 was photographed at Adelaide in October 1958 just after the GNR Board had been dissolved and its locomotives shared between the UTA and CIE. The former had not wasted any time in putting their initials on the engine's buffer beam. One member of this class, No 131, was preserved by CIE in the 1960s.** Dennis Bates

Bottom: **The S class of the GNR must surely be one of the most elegant and handsomely proportioned designs ever to grace the railways of these islands. Built between 1913 and 1915 and completely renewed in the late 1930s, Clifford's masterpiece is represented here by No 190 _Lugnaquilla_, obviously not long out of the works, being recorded at Portadown on 29th July 1953 on the 3.15pm semi-fast from Belfast to Dublin.** A D Hutchinson

Top: **The continuity which was such a factor in GNR locomotive practice is perhaps best illustrated by the example of the U class. The first of these 4-4-0s were introduced by Glover in 1915. When the need for some new light 4-4-0s was felt after the Second World War the 1915 design was revived by McIntosh. The second batch had a slightly higher boiler pressure and a more enclosed cab with a distinctive large side window. No 201 *Meath*, the first of the 1948 engines, is seen here on shed at Enniskillen in the summer of 1957.**
Midland Publishing collection

Centre right: **The now preserved V class Compound 4-4-0 No 85 *Merlin* is seen at Adelaide in the early 1960s. Introduced in 1932 by Glover, the Compounds were a break with GNR tradition, the first engines of this type to run on the railway. The rebuilding of the Boyne viaduct at Drogheda, which was completed at this time, enabled these heavier and more powerful machines to be used on the main line. As built, the Compounds had round topped fireboxes later replaced by the same type of boiler and Belpaire firebox as those used on the VS class.** R C Ludgate

Bottom right: **A fine portrait of VS class 4-4-0 UTA No 58 (GNR No 208) *Lagan*, at the GNR shed at Amiens Street in Dublin on 15th April 1961. Slightly more powerful than the Compounds the VS class display once again the continuity of GNR loco design, of which they were the final flowering.** Des FitzGerald

TANK LOCOMOTIVES

Left: The GNR had several types of tank engine on its books. The same principles were followed with these as was the case with the tender engines. The JT class 2-4-2 tanks, of which No 91 is an example, seen here at Clones shed in 1957, were derivatives of the J class 4-4-0s built in the 1880s. The JT's long outlived the tender engines they were based on, the latter had all been withdrawn by 1924.
Midland Publishing collection

Above: No 22 was the first of the four RT class 0-6-4 tanks built between 1908 and 1911 by Beyer Peacock. They were designed for use on the dock lines around Belfast where some clearances were very tight. No 22 is at Adelaide in this view taken around 1957.
Midland Publishing collection.

Left: The GNR's most numerous type was the 4-4-2 tanks of the T1 and T2 classes built from 1913 through to 1929 to Glover's design. Based on the U class 4-4-0s they were found on station pilot and local passenger services around the system though in our period they tended to congregate at either end of the Belfast to Dublin main line. No 189, one of the first batch of T1s built by Beyer Peacock in 1913, is on station pilot duty at Amiens Street station in Dublin on 6th August 1958.
Keith Walton

0-6-0 GOODS ENGINES

Right: **The 0-6-0 tender engine was used by virtually every Irish railway for its goods traffic and the GNR was no exception. Types dating back to the 1880s were still active in the 1950s and '60s. The A class 0-6-0s were introduced by J C Park in 1882. No 150, seen at Adelaide on 5th September 1954, was built in 1890. Park, Locomotive Superintendent and CME from 1881 to 1894 came to the Irish Great Northern from the English railway of the same name. Among many achievements he set out the distinctive GNR 'house style' which made every locomotive recognisable as belonging to the company.** R Tourret

Above: **An improved version of the A class was introduced by Park in 1893. The AL class had a higher boiler pressure and a greater tractive effort. No 59, built by Beyer Peacock in 1894 and originally named *Kilkenny*, was still going strong when photographed at Enniskillen shed in August 1957.**

Midland Publishing collection

Right: **The PG class was the 0-6-0 variant of the P class 4-4-0s. One of the last survivors, No 10, built in 1904 at Dundalk, heads a goods at the Liverpool shed on Donegal Quay in Belfast on 3rd March 1961. This locomotive was rebuilt with a superheated boiler in 1925 making it a PGs class engine.** John Laird

Left: Among the most powerful 0-6-0s possessed by the GNR were the 30 locomotives of the SG, SG2 and SG3 classes, built between 1913 and 1921. With boilers and cylinders similar to those used on the S class 4-4-0s, the SGs had 5ft 1in driving wheels, which were large enough to give the locos a fair turn of speed if called upon to work the occasional passenger service. SG class, UTA No 43 (GNR No 175), here paired with a tender off one of the 1948 batch of U or UG class locomotives, heads a long northbound goods near the border on the former GNR main line in 1964. Bryan Boyle

Above: SG2 No 40 (GNR No 18) was built by Nasmyth Wilson in 1924. It is shunting some of the GNR's brown liveried vacuum braked wagons which could be used on passenger trains, at the south end of Portadown station on 5th July 1961. Des FitzGerald

Left: The GNR's last 0-6-0 design was the UG class dating from 1937. Though based on the U class 4-4-0 this example of a 0-6-0 following a 4-4-0 design did not materialise for 22 years after the original. The UGs were really mixed traffic locomotives which were often seen on passenger trains. UTA No 49 (GNR No 149) was one of the second batch built in 1948 and had the distinction of being the very last 0-6-0 delivered to an Irish railway. Midland Publishing collection

THE MAIN LINE

We will now embark on a photographic journey around the GNR system beginning at Belfast on the main line and heading south towards Dublin.

Right: **This remarkable bird's eye view of Great Victoria Street station in Belfast was taken in September 1964 by Craig Robb. Among the many landmarks which can be spotted are the Opera House in the bottom right hand corner and the GNR Grosvenor Road goods depot in the centre of the picture. Great Victoria Street station was closed in April 1976 when Belfast Central, a name singularly inappropriate for a station on the site of a former goods yard about a mile from the city centre, was opened. However wiser counsels are now prevailing and a new station at Great Victoria Street, five minutes walk from the City Hall will open in 1995, with the line from there to Central Junction being rebuilt.**

Below: **In UTA days S class 4-4-0 No 60 (GNR No 172)** *Slieve Donard* **looking surprisingly clean in her UTA lined black livery, prepares to leave platform 4 of Great Victoria Street station with the 1.05pm, Saturdays only, Belfast to Portadown service, on 11th November 1961.** John Laird

Top: **To the south of the station outside the overall roof was a single faced platform known as 'the motor platform' which had been used decades before by the GNR's short-lived steam rail motors on suburban services to Lisburn. WT class 2-6-4 tank No 51 has the road from this platform in this 1965 view.** Midland Publishing collection

Above: **A pair of ex-LMS NCC WT class 2-6-4 tank engines, Nos 56 and 55, are seen in the carriage sidings at Great Victoria Street on 28th August 1965. To the right of the picture are the UTA's first AEC railcars, Nos 6 and 7, which were running as a 2-car set on the GNR line at this time.** Richard Whitford

CENTRAL JUNCTION

Above: **On 15th September 1962, RT 0-6-4 tank UTA No 24 (GNR No 166) shunts goods wagons at Central Junction, a short distance out from Great Victoria Street station. The line to the right led to Maysfields goods depot and over the River Lagan to make a connection with the former Belfast & County Down Railway system at Ballymacarrett Junction, and over dock lines to the LMS NCC at York Road. This is the route followed by trains today to reach Belfast Central station. When the 'new' Great Victoria Street station is opened, there will be a triangular junction here to enable trains from Bangor, Larne and Londonderry to reach the new station.** John Laird

ADELAIDE

Right: **The Great Northern's largest shed was at Adelaide, 1½ miles out from the terminus. Opened in March 1911, it replaced the original UR shed at Great Victoria Street. One very unusual feature for such a large shed may be observed in Craig Robb's aerial view of it: the triangle to the left of the site on which engines were turned. For some inexplicable reason Adelaide was never equipped with a turntable.**

Top: **On 14th April 1960 GNR V class Compounds No 85 _Merlin_, nearest the camera, and No 86 _Peregrine_ were on shed. The arches in the background enabled wagons of loco coal to be taken to the coaling stage.** Des FitzGerald

Above: **Richard Whitford's atmospheric photograph taken on 2nd March 1963, shows two LMS NCC Moguls, Nos 93 _The Foyle_ and 98 _King Edward VIII_, and a pair of GNR S class engines, No 62 (GNR No 190) _Lugnaquilla_ and No 60 (GNR No 172) _Slieve Donard_, on shed.**

Top: **Moving out of Belfast, there was always a healthy suburban traffic from the stations along the Lagan valley to Lisburn. U class 4-4-0 No 202 *Louth* passes Finaghy station, which opened in 1907, with a train from Antrim to Belfast, on 6th May 1959.** J G Dewing

Above: **T2 class 4-4-2 tank No 116, built by Nasmyth Wilson in 1924, brings a stopping service, probably from Armagh, into Lisburn in the summer of 1957.** Midland Publishing collection

Above: **On 29th August 1964, 2-6-4T No 55 passes Moira station with a Belfast bound train. The buildings at Moira on the up platform date back to the opening of the Ulster Railway in the 1840s and are the only early UR station buildings still extant.** Bryan Boyle

Centre left: **The working of train services through Lurgan has always been complicated by the presence of two level crossings just beyond the station in the down (Belfast) direction and this one at the end of the station platforms in the other direction. On 22nd August 1962 U class No 68 (GNR No 205) *Down* leaves Lurgan with the 11.15am special to Portadown.** Des FitzGerald

Below: **In May 1957 U class 4-4-0 No 198 *Lough Swilly* nears Portadown on a train from Warrenpoint to Belfast. This was one of the first batch of Us built in 1915. No 198 was only named in 1950, having run anonymously for the previously 35 years.** A D Hutchinson

Opposite page top: **On 6th July 1963 VS class No 58 (GNR No 208) *Lagan* comes off a train for Derry at Portadown to be replaced by S class No 170 *Errigal* for the rest of the journey. The weight of the VS class restricted them to the main line.** Des FitzGerald

Opposite page centre: **On Thursday 29th July 1965, WT class No 56 was recorded on the 2.45pm train from Dublin to Belfast at Drumbanagher between Goraghwood and Poyntzpass.** Bryan Boyle

Opposite page bottom: **SG3 class 0-6-0 No 36 (GNR No 49) starts a heavy goods out of Goraghwood station in March 1964.** Craig Robb

Top: **WT class 2-6-4T No 50 passes through Bessbrook station some 43 miles from Belfast, with a Dublin bound train on 5th July 1961. Northern Ireland Railways opened a new station to serve Newry on this site on 14th May 1984. The town of Newry seems to be gradually expanding up the hill towards its new station.** Des FitzGerald

Above: **On 29th August 1964, WT 2-6-4T No 1 struggles past the summit of the line with a Dundalk to Portadown goods train consisting of 44 wagons. The photographer, Bryan Boyle, recalls that the locomotive had previously slipped to a standstill at Adavoyle despite the apparently fine weather and dry rails. No 1 was not the first of the WTs but was one of the second batch built by the LMS at Derby in 1947.**

DUNDALK

Above: **An interesting combination of GNR and NCC motive power head a return special to Belfast out of Dundalk station on 19th July 1962. GNR S class No 171 *Slieve Gullion* built by Beyer Peacock in 1913 and completely renewed at Dundalk works in 1938, pilots LMS NCC W class 2-6-0 No 104, which was built in Belfast in 1942. No 104 was the last member of the class to be constructed and one of only two not to be named – the other was No 102, which was withdrawn in 1956, after a career of only 16 years.** Des FitzGerald

Centre right: **The last of the VS class to survive, No 207 *Boyne,* leaves Dundalk with a train for Belfast in 1965 – the year of its withdrawal.** Craig Robb

Right: **A reminder that Dundalk was where the GNR had its works. The first locomotive was built here in 1887 and the last, UG class 0-6-0 No 82, in 1937, though it could be argued that the rebuilding of the S class at Dundalk in 1938/39 created virtually new locomotives making them the last 'new' engines to emerge from the works. Parked alongside the main line, on 16th August 1953 fresh from overhaul and awaiting tenders, are QLGs class 0-6-0 No 108 and Qs class 4-4-0 No 130. This picture also provides an interesting illustration of the GNR practice of having a 0-6-0 variant of its 4-4-0 designs.** R Tourret

Top: **On the 8th September 1962 GNR Compound No 85 *Merlin* pauses with a southbound stopping train consisting of a train of stock in the then recently introduced CIE black and orange livery, at Dunleer between Dundalk and Drogheda.** Des FitzGerald

Above: **VS class 4-4-0 No 207 *Boyne* roars through Malahide station on 22nd July 1965 with a train from Belfast. Malahide is some 9 miles out from the GNR terminus in Dublin and immediately north of the station the line crosses an inlet of the sea on low viaducts and causeways.** Craig Robb

AMIENS STREET STATION, DUBLIN

Top: **Towards the end of the GNR era in August 1958, a train of AEC railcars arrives at the station from Howth. Today, CIE diesels have replaced the GNR steam locomotives in the engine shed.** Midland Publishing collection

Above: **A few years later with CIE firmly in control, S class No 174 *Carrantuohill* heads a train in CIE's attractive green livery, out of the Howth platform at the station.**
David Murray

THE IRISH NORTH

The lines west from Dundalk to Clones, Enniskillen, Omagh and Derry along with the branch to Bundoran had been worked by the Irish North Western Railway up to its incorporation in the newly formed GNR in the 1870s. This line was joined at Clones by the Ulster Railway route extended from its original 1848 terminus at Armagh to reach Monaghan in 1858 and Clones in 1863. The government of Northern Ireland destroyed these lines in 1957 when they decided to close those sections of the route which lay within their jurisdiction. The UR line was closed from Portadown to the border as was the section from Omagh to Enniskillen along with the Bundoran branch, most of which lay within Northern Ireland. CIE maintained freight and parcels services on the sections within the Irish Republic to serve Clones, Cavan and Monaghan for a couple of years but the action of the Northern Ireland government effectively killed the whole system. The rump which remained in the Republic could never be viable once the through routes had been truncated.

Below: **At Dundalk the junction of the lines to Clones and beyond with the GNR main line was just south of the station. AL class 0-6-0 No 55 is shunting at the junction on 2nd August 1958.** Keith Walton

Bottom: **Clones station, until the previous year a major junction with services to Dublin, Belfast and Derry and daily host to one of Ireland's few named trains, the 'Bundoran Express' is already, by August 1958, a shadow of its former self, a stopping place on a system which has had its heart and purpose destroyed. The GNR railcar and trailer are on a parcels working from Cavan.** Keith Walton

ENNISKILLEN SHED

Top: **Turning away from the sadness of the previous picture let us recall the Irish North at its best in the following pages. Two of the classes long associated with these lines are seen at the shed at Enniskillen. On the left is 1915-built U class 4-4-0 No 197** *Lough Neagh*. **Beside the U is Ps class 4-4-0 No 73 dating from 1895. This was one of the members of this class with the larger 6ft 6in driving wheels. The line passing the shed and the elevated Enniskillen South signal cabin in the centre of the picture is that to Clones, that to the right is the Sligo, Leitrim & Northern Counties route to Sligo (see chapter 3).**
Midland Publishing collection

Centre right: **1948 built U class No 204** *Antrim* **stands beside one of her elderly sisters. When the locomotives of the GNR Board were divided in October 1958, No 204 went to CIE.**
Midland Publishing collection

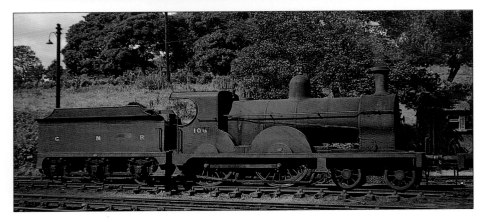

Bottom right: **PPs No 106 was built in 1906 by Beyer Peacock whose distinctive red builders' plate can be seen on the splasher of the leading driving wheel. The 4-4-0 was originally named** *Tornado*. Midland Publishing collection

ENNISKILLEN STATION

Above: **The pride of the line was the Irish North's very own named train, the 'Bundoran Express'. An up working eases round the** sharp curve into Enniskillen station in August 1957, hauled, with steam to spare, by U class 4-4-0 No 199 *Lough Derg*. The term express was used rather loosely when applied to this train. The 1952 GNR timetable shows that it left Dublin at 8.45am and did not cover the 160 miles to Bundoran until 2.00pm.

Below: **U class No 197 *Lough Neagh* prepares to leave Enniskillen in August 1957 with a train for Omagh. Rail services to Enniskillen ended the month after these photographs were taken.** Both Midland Publishing collection

THE BUNDORAN BRANCH

This line was frequented by holiday-makers bound for the seaside, pilgrims going to the holy island on Lough Derg near Pettigo and amateur smugglers galore!

Above: **Ps class 4-4-0 No 73 leaves Fintona Junction with an Omagh to Enniskillen train in July 1954. This would have connected with an Enniskillen to Bundoran train at Bundoran Junction.** A D Hutchinson

Below: **Bundoran Junction had a triangular layout allowing through running from Bundoran to either Omagh or Enniskillen. U class 4-4-0 No 204 *Antrim* is shunting a through Belfast to Bundoran carriage onto the front of a Bundoran bound train at the junction in August 1957.** Midland Publishing collection

Above: **The first station on the branch to the west of the junction was Irvinestown. Ps class 4-4-0 No 73 arrives at the station with a train from Bundoran in the last summer of the line's operation.**
Midland Publishing collection

Below: **The line crossed into the Irish Republic and County Donegal after leaving Belleek. At Ballyshannon, the first and only station in the** Republic before the terminus was reached, Irish customs officials examined trains arriving from Northern Ireland. The hut and table on the platform opposite the train were for their use. The GNR station at Ballyshannon was on the opposite side of the town to that of the County Donegal narrow gauge branch from Donegal Town. On 6th September 1957, during the last month of services on the line, the 10.30am from Bundoran arrives behind 1911-built PPs 4-4-0 No 44. Keith Walton

THE DERRY ROAD

Top right: **The next part of our Great Northern odyssey takes us along the line from Portadown Junction to Derry. Tunnels were comparatively rare on the Irish railway network but there was one on this line on the Portadown side of Dungannon station. It was built at the insistence of the local landowner and scared the living daylights out of me when I first travelled through it as a very young child. S class No 174** *Carrantuohill* **leaves the tunnel with the 3.00pm Belfast to Derry train on 28th August 1964.** Des FitzGerald

Centre right: **On the very damp and dreary morning of 19th July 1963 SG class 0-6-0 No 43 (GNR No 175) arrives at Dungannon with the 4.30am goods from Omagh to Portadown.** Richard Whitford

Below: **U class No 67 (GNR No202)** *Louth* **stands at Dungannon station having just brought in the 2.35pm local service from Portadown, on 31st August 1963. Dungannon's signalbox was located on the station's main platform. This was a quite unusual arrangement, though it was also to be seen at Cavan where the GNR shared a station with the MGWR.**
Des FitzGerald

Above: **Between Dungannon and Omagh, trains in both directions faced a formidable climb over the watershed of the Sperrin Mountains. The stiffest test was reserved for trains bound for Belfast on the stretch beyond Carrickmore station, known logically as Carrickmore bank, where the gradient was as steep as 1 in 72. S class 4-4-0 No 60 (GNR No 172)** *Slieve Donard* **is hard at work on the bank with the 12.55pm train from Derry on 24th August 1963.** Des FitzGerald

Left: **My personal nostalgia trip begins here. About a mile out of Omagh station in the direction of Dungannon, a branch diverged to a goods depot in the town's Market Yard. This junction was the scene of a potentially serious derailment in March 1933 when the junction points were tampered with causing a mixed Dungannon to Derry train to leave the track. This was one of two malicious derailments which occurred during the bitter railway strike of that year. I spent hours there as a boy watching the Omagh engine shunting at this depot. On 20th July 1962 SG2 class 0-6-0 No 40 (GNR No 18) was the engine on duty.** Richard Whitford

Opposite page top: **The GNR Foyle Road station in Derry had a somewhat Italianate style to it, shades of the Amiens Street terminus in Dublin on a more modest scale perhaps.** Derek Young

Opposite page bottom: **In August 1963 the now preserved S class No 171 *Slieve Gullion* starts her train out of Foyle Road Station. In 1963 the UTA found itself with a chronic engine shortage. In an attempt to ease this the Authority bought four ex-GNR locomotives from CIE. These engines, S class 4-4-0s Nos 170 *Errigal*, 171 *Slieve Gullion*, 174 *Carrantuohill* and VS class No 207 *Boyne*, retained their GNR numbers and blue livery which CIE had not altered. The move north ensured that No 171 survived long enough to be saved by the embryonic Railway Preservation Society of Ireland. Today the Foyle Valley Railway Museum stands on this site and 3ft gauge tracks have been laid in order to run the museum's preserved CDR stock.** Craig Robb

LISBURN TO ANTRIM

The 20 mile long branch from Knockmore Junction on the GNR main line just south of Lisburn to the NCC main line at Antrim is still open and at the time of writing carries Northern Ireland Railway's services from Belfast to Londonderry, though these trains will shortly revert to the revived NCC line east of Antrim. The branch has for long been a vital link between the GNR and the NCC systems.

Top right: **In April 1968 an unidentified WT works a ballast train through Crumlin.** Derek Young

Centre right: **The only way to get the larger GNR section locomotives to the UTA's works at York Road for attention was via the Antrim branch. This was the explanation for the unlikely sight of VS class 4-4-0 No 58 (GNR No 208) *Lagan* passing the typically GNR signal box at Ballinderry on 11th July 1963.** Des FitzGerald

Bottom right: **Following the end of passenger services on the branch in 1960 a speed limit of 25mph was imposed and the line was only used for the transfer of stock and the occasional special train. When the Derry Road closed in February 1965 CIE began to operate a scheduled nightly goods service from Dundalk to Derry over the branch. This meant that the track had to be upgraded and kept in decent condition. On Wednesday 31st March 1965, a permanent way gang engaged on this work enjoy a welcome break in the spring sunshine, with WT No 55 simmering gently in the background.** Craig Robb

NEWRY TO WARRENPOINT

The branch to Newry and Warrenpoint left the GNR main line at Goraghwood. Originally the line had continued to Armagh through Ireland's longest railway tunnel at Lissummon and down that fateful incline on which Ireland's worst ever railway disaster occurred in 1889. The branch closed in 1965 though today Newry is served by a new station on the main line (see page 66).

Above: **On 13th July 1963 U class 4-4-0 No 68 (GNR No 205)** *Down* **stands on the up main line at Goraghwood having shunted the stock of a special out of the station, as an unidentified SG class 0-6-0 arrives with a train off the branch.** John Langford

Below: **UG 0-6-0 No 49 (GNR No 149) crosses the Newry Canal and heads for Newry Dublin Bridge station with empty coaching stock bound for Warrenpoint on 29th August 1964.** Bryan Boyle

Opposite page top: **For much of its length south of Newry the branch followed the banks of the tidal Clanrye River. At Narrow Water S class No 60 (GNR No 172)** *Slieve Donard* **hurries along the 4.15pm train from Warrenpoint to Belfast on 13th July 1963.** John Laird

Opposite page centre: **Warrenpoint station was built with the attractive yellow glazed bricks of which the GNR made extensive use. On 4th July 1961 U class No 65 (GNR No 200)** *Lough Melvin*, **in blue with a mahogany liveried coach behind, proudly flies the old company's flag three years into the UTA era. At this time the UTA had two engines bearing this name, the other being the former Sligo, Leitrim & Northern Counties 0-6-4 tank.** Des FitzGerald

Opposite page bottom: **On summer Sundays and Bank Holidays a great deal of excursion traffic was attracted to the seaside at Warrenpoint. The four return excursions in John Langford's picture, taken on Sunday 14th July 1963, are all headed by ex-GNR locomotives. These are UG class 0-6-0 No 45 (GNR No 78), U class 4-4-0 No 68 (GNR No 205)** *Down* **and two S class engines, No 60 (GNR No 172)** *Slieve Donard* **and No 174** *Carrantuohill*.

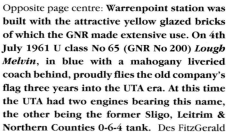

GREAT NORTHERN BRANCH LINES

Top right: **Three of the less well known GNR branches are pictured on this page. The line from Dungannon to Cookstown was opened in 1879 and finally closed with the Derry Road in 1965 though latterly it was open for freight only and since 1959, as far as Coalisland only. The GNR station at Cookstown was alongside that of the NCC line from Cookstown Junction on the Belfast York Road to Londonderry Waterside main line. There was a connection between the two stations. What looks like a QLG class 0-6-0 was at the GNR's Cookstown station in August 1957.**
Midland Publishing collection

Centre: **The 6½ mile branch, from Inniskeen Junction on the Dundalk to Clones line, to Carrickmacross, opened in 1886 and though it lost its passenger services in 1947 it remained open for goods traffic until 1959. This 1957 view shows the single platform with its overall roof which was typical of a number of GNR branch termini.** Midland Publishing Collection

Bottom: **A branch 39 miles long ran from Drogheda through Navan and Kells to Oldcastle. The passenger service was often provided by a railcar or a railbus but on this occasion, in August 1957, SG2 0-6-0 No 15 is seen arriving at Oldcastle with a train from Drogheda.**
Midland Publishing collection

GREAT NORTHERN
DIESELS

Top: **The GNR was one of the first railways in the British Isles to make serious use of diesel traction, aware of the savings which could be obtained by employing diesel railcars and railbuses on lightly trafficked lines. The first of these vehicles, railcar A, seen here at Omagh as UTA No 101 in May 1960, was built at Dundalk works in 1932.** J G Dewing

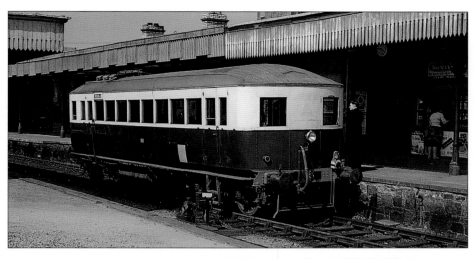

Centre: **Railcar C1, recorded at Enniskillen in August 1957, coupled to one of the parcels and luggage trailers built for use with the railcars, was put into service in 1934. Powered by a 96hp Gardner diesel engine, its engine and driving compartment were articulated from the passenger saloon. Railcar C1 was similar in concept to the vehicles being built at around the same time for the CDR narrow gauge system.** Midland Publishing collection

Below: **Built in 1936 as railcar E and seen here at Newry Edward Street station in September 1964 as UTA No 104, the diesel engine was contained in a 6-wheeled section in the middle of the unit from which the two passenger saloons were articulated.** Neil Sprinks

Left: **The quirkiest elements of the GNR's diesel fleet were the railbuses, literally road buses converted to run on rails using the Howden-Meredith wheels combining a steel flange with a rubber tyre, as seen on this example photographed at Dundalk works in 1957.**
Midland Publishing collection

Below: **Access to the vehicle was through a door at the rear of the saloon. The steps off the railbuses' platforms enabled them to pick up passengers at level crossings where no conventional platform existed. This railbus photographed at Drogheda was in service on the Oldcastle branch.** F W Shuttleworth

Left: **Lack of resources rather than a lack of understanding of the potential benefits of dieselisation meant that this German built MAK diesel supplied to the GNRB in 1954 was the only GNR diesel locomotive. The 8-wheeled machine was an 800hp diesel hydraulic; it weighed 57½ tons and had a maximum speed of 53mph. Numbered 800 by the GNRB and seen here at Dundalk on 29th August 1958, at the time of writing, the remains of this historic machine, surely a worthy candidate for preservation, languishes in a scrapyard in County Galway.** Cyril Fry/H Stacpoole collection

Above: **In 1948 the GNR placed an order for 20 diesel railcars with AEC Limited of Southall, who had built the successful railcars introduced by the Great Western Railway in the 1930s. They were formed into three coach trains with an unpowered converted coach in the middle and a power car at each end. An attractive dark blue and cream livery was applied to the new railcars. No 602 heads a typical 3-coach formation at Tynan on the Armagh to Clones line on 23rd August 1957.**
Midland Publishing collection

Below: **No 615 heads a 2-coach formation, without the trailer in the middle, into Amiens Street station in Dublin in the summer of 1957. The bodies of these railcars, built by Park Royal, had seats for 12 first class and 32 third class passengers as well as accommodation for luggage and the guard.** F W Shuttleworth

Above: **The final types of GNR railcars were those designed by British United Traction Limited (BUT) and assembled at Dundalk. The BUT vehicles of the 700 and 900 series were supplied to the GNRB in 1957/58. The 900s, which had a driving cab at only one end like the 600s, were designed for use in formations of up to eight cars in conjunction with the 700 series, which had a driving compartment and a corridor connection at each end. These and unpowered trailers made up the rest of the train. In this view of a Derry to Belfast train at Strabane in 1958, a 900 railcar still in GNR blue and cream livery but dis-** playing UTA crests, distinguished from the 600s by the roof headlight, leads the formation. The second and fourth vehicles are 700 series railcars with the third and fifth carriages being unpowered trailers. The final carriage is probably another 900. Keith Bannister

Below: **In August 1958 a BUT 700 series railcar showing the corridor connection and the driver's compartment which it had at both ends, is seen at Foyle Road station in Derry.** Cyril Fry / H Stacpoole collection

Chapter Three

THE SLIGO, LEITRIM & NORTHERN

COUNTIES RAILWAY

This short chapter is being devoted to that most Irish of railways the SLNCR which also had the dubious distinction of being the last independent standard gauge railway in the British Isles. The company was incorporated in 1875 and opened its line linking the GNR at Enniskillen to the MGWR at Collooney near Sligo, in stages between 1879 and 1882. It served some of the most sparsely populated parts of the north of Ireland, where the land was poor. In a predominantly agricultural country like Ireland the prosperity of an area was largely determined by this inheritance from nature.

The very essence of the SLNCR is expressed in this delightful image of 0-6-4T *Sir Henry* with a long cattle train bound for Enniskillen, recorded at Belcoo on 15th August 1957.
Midland Publishing collection

The SLNCR joined the MGWR Dublin to Sligo line at Carrignagat Junction near Collooney and had running powers from there over the 5½ miles of track into Sligo. There was also a connection at Collooney with the erstwhile Waterford, Limerick & Western route from Sligo to Claremorris. The headquarters and workshops of the SLNCR were at Manorhamilton which was roughly half way along the line.

Never very prosperous, the SLNCR was dependent on its two powerful neighbours, especially the GNR at Enniskillen, as outlets for its traffic. A plan whereby the MGWR and the GNR considered buying the line in 1894 came to nought.

Because it straddled the border it escaped the clutches of the GSR in 1925 and the UTA on its formation in 1948. Its main traffic for many years was cattle which were shipped from the west along the SLNCR for export to Britain through the ports of Belfast and Derry. Though it received subsidies from both governments it carried on in its own distinctive way until the closure of the GNR lines to Enniskillen in 1957, at the insistence of the government of Northern Ireland.

At a stroke this removed its *raison d'être* and led to its last train running on 30th September 1957. It is ironic that it was the emasculation of the once powerful GNR at the hands of a clique of small minded, unimaginative and anti-railway Ulster politicians that led in the end to the demise of the SLNCR.

The particular charm of the SLNCR attracted many visiting British enthusiasts. Even though it closed in 1957 many aspects of the line have been recorded in colour for posterity.

Left: **The SLNCR locomotive fleet in the 1950s consisted entirely of 0-6-4 tanks, the last tender engine having been withdrawn in 1949. Two of the oldest survivors were *Lissadell* (see *Irish Railways in Colour: From Steam to Diesel 1955-1967,* page 66) and *Hazlewood,* seen here at Manorhamilton on 29th June 1957. Like all SLNCR engines they are known by name only and never numbered. *Lissadell* was withdrawn in 1954 but lasted until 1957. *Hazlewood* remained in use longer, and was still in the traffic stock when the railway closed in 1957.** Neil Sprinks

Below: ***Sir Henry,* built by Beyer Peacock in 1904, an enlarged and improved version of the earlier 0-6-4Ts, is seen here shunting the inevitable cattle wagon, at Enniskillen on 4th September 1957.** Keith Walton

Top left: The only engineering feature of any significance on the line was the Killyhevlin or Weir's bridge, which took the line over the waterway connecting the upper and lower parts of Lough Erne, just outside Enniskillen. Keith Walton

Top right: Manorhamilton station from the front window of a railbus arriving from Enniskillen. The goods is the 11.15am from Sligo to Enniskillen headed by one of the last two engines acquired by the SLNCR, *Lough Melvin,* which along with its sister *Lough Erne,* was actually built in 1949 but only secured by the railway on hire purchase from Beyer Peacock as late as 1951. Keith Walton.

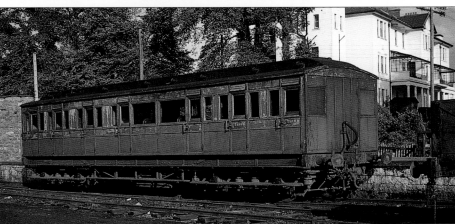

Centre right: In 1924 the SLNCR acquired three bogie coaches, previous passenger vehicles having been 6-wheelers. These were tricomposites with accommodation for all three classes of passengers. As there was only one first class compartment this was divided into smoking and non-smoking sections by a central sliding partition. Recorded in 1957 in its faded SLNCR brown/maroon livery, it should be pointed out that this picture of the carriage is not printed the wrong way round; the door handles *were* on the left.
Keith Bannister

Right: The SLNCR's railcar B was built by Walkers of Wigan in 1947. It was in effect a scaled up version, the only one to run on the broad gauge, of the railcars which this firm had been building since the 1930s for the CDR. Like many rural Irish lines which had to be built as cheaply as possible, there were many level crossings on the SLNCR. Railcar B is in the Glenfarne to Belcoo section with a Sligo to Enniskillen working in May 1957. At this point three level crossings were located very close together. The railcar is approaching level crossing No 9 at Thornhill; the signal in the 'off' position which it is passing in fact protects the next crossing beyond the one in the picture. J G Dewing

Above: **Two more views of railcar B here await-ing departure at Sligo station in 1957. This Walker railcar, unlike those built for the nar-row gauge, could be driven from either end.**
F W Shuttleworth

Centre left: **Railcar B outside the small SLNCR shed at Enniskillen in 1957. The engine unit is at the end nearest the camera and was articu-lated from the passenger saloon.**
Keith Bannister

Bottom: **When the SLNCR closed in 1957, rail-car B was acquired by CIE. Numbered 2509 it was used on the Ballybrophy to Limerick branch and also on driver training duties on the former GNR main line. In the company of diesel shunter E430 it is seen here at Amiens Street shed in Dublin on 24th August 1970.**
Denis Bates

Opposite page top: **The SLNCR used several railbuses based on the GNR pattern over the years. Catching the evening sun in the SLNCR bay platform at Enniskillen is railbus 2A, with its diminutive luggage trailer behind it.**
Keith Bannister

Opposite page bottom: **Railbus A, seen at Glen-farne in May 1957, was built by the GNR at Dundalk in 1935 and later sold to the SLNCR. Its trailer was built at the SLNCR shops at Manorhamilton on the frame of an ex-GSR Sentinel locomotive.** J G Dewing

Above: **Two views of SLNCR steam locomotives at work conclude this short survey of a fascinating concern. On 4th September 1957 *Sir Henry* brings the 2.15pm goods from Enniskillen into Manorhamilton.** Keith Walton

Below: **On 27th May 1957 0-6-4 tank *Enniskillen*, built by Beyer Peacock in 1905, pauses for water and lubrication at Manorhamilton. The tricomposite bogie coach tucked on at the end of the string of goods and cattle wagons behind the engine was being worked empty from Sligo to Enniskillen. It would form the passenger accommodation on the 7.20pm mixed train from Enniskillen that evening.** J G Dewing

Chapter Four

THE LEGACY OF THE LMS

This chapter explores the influence which the biggest of the post grouping British railway companies, the London Midland & Scottish Railway, exerted on the Irish railway scene. It really reflects the involvement in Ireland of two of its constituents, the Midland Railway and the London & North Western Railway, which went back many years before the formation of the LMS at the grouping of Britain's railways in 1923.

In the nineteenth century, when all of Ireland was part of the United Kingdom, it was inevitable that British railway companies should take an interest in railway developments in Ireland. This often revolved around getting a share of the lucrative goods traffic to the ports on the British side of the Irish Sea. The growth of ports such as Fishguard, Holyhead, Heysham and Stranraer owed much to the railway companies. The first of the British companies to get involved on the ground in Ireland itself was the LNWR with its own station at the North Wall

in Dublin and a heavy financial commitment to the Dundalk, Newry & Greenore Railway. Both of these LNWR ventures were directly linked to the cross channel traffic.

It was from the activities of the Midland Railway that the most obvious manifestation of the influence of the LMS in Ireland was to arise. The MR became a significant player on the Irish railway scene when it acquired Ireland's fourth largest railway, the Belfast & Northern Counties in 1903. The MR influence was extended in 1906 when jointly, with the GNR(I), it bought the Donegal Railway. The MR did not seem to interfere greatly with its Irish broad gauge satellite which was managed in Belfast by the Northern Counties Committee of the parent company. BNCR locomotive practice was continued without any recognisable input from the MR works at Derby.

This seemed to change at the grouping and in the years that followed it was possible to see the influence of Derby works in the

design of the new locomotives built for the LMS NCC lines in Ulster. This led to the NCC having the most modern fleet of steam locomotives in Ireland, which was inherited by the UTA in 1948. The final survivors of these Derby inspired engines were the last steam locomotives at work in these islands.

Below: **Though joint owners of the County Donegal narrow gauge system, the branch from Victoria Road station in Londonderry to Strabane was wholly owned by the MR and later the LMS though worked of course by the County Donegal Railways Joint Committee which ran the whole system. The permanent way inspector based at Waterside station had responsibility for the upkeep of the track and by all accounts it was by far the best on the whole of the CDR. Class 5A 2-6-4 tank No 1** *Alice* **leaves the LMS' second and perhaps less well known station in Londonderry in October 1953.** Colour Rail

Above: **A D Hutchinson's photographs of the line were taken in 1950 and 1951. On 13th July 1950 0-6-0 saddle tank No 3 *Dundalk*, built at Crewe in 1873, retaining its red LNWR number-plate to the end and a train of coaches in LNWR chocolate and white livery, are seen at Greenore.**

THE DUNDALK, NEWRY & GREENORE RAILWAY

Up until its closure in 1951 the DN&G was like a part of the London & North Western Railway which time forgot. It was as if the grouping in 1923, which saw the demise of the LNWR in Britain, had never happened. Crewe-built saddle tanks dating back to the 1870s hauled trains of 6-wheelers in LNWR livery past LNWR signals, as if in a time warp. The first part of the line from Dundalk to Greenore was opened in 1873. A second line along the shore of Carlingford Lough, from Greenore to Newry, was added in 1876. The intention of the DN&G was to develop the port of Greenore at the tip of Carlingford Lough. The LNWR was heavily involved financially in building the port and the railway lines to connect it to both Dundalk and Newry. The port and the railways were never very successful. Passenger steamers ceased to run in 1926, by which time ownership had passed on to the LMS, and though freight, especially livestock, remained at quite respectable levels, the railway was losing money from the 1920s onwards. Its prospects were not improved by the partition of Ireland which meant that traffic on the line to Newry was subject to customs examination. From 1933 the GNR took over the working of the lines which resulted in some economies but the system retained its essentially LNWR character, until closure in 1951.

Above: **A close up of the 6-wheel carriages seen in the previous picture. I suspect that these are probably the only authentic colour pictures in existence of what was the livery of Britain's self styled 'Premier Line'.**

Left: **The line from Greenore to Newry must have been one of the most picturesque stretches of track in Ireland. It ran along the shores of Carlingford Lough with the mountains of Mourne forming a shore backdrop on the other side of the lough. A GNR JT class 2-4-2 tank hurries a train of LNWR 6-wheelers towards Newry on 27th July 1951.**

U2 CLASS

Top: **Like all Irish railways the NCC relied heavily on 4-4-0s. For many years the BNCR had built Compounds of the Von Borries system which the company's engineer Bowman** Malcolm applied to locomotives on both the broad and narrow gauges. By the 1930s compounding had fallen out of favour at York Road and new 4-4-0s were simple expansion machines. U2 class 4-4-0 No 85 was built in Belfast in 1934. Unlike many of her sisters she was never given a name. A number of Derby inspired features like the dome and the Fowler chimney can be observed. Seen at Larne in September 1954, No 85 lasted until 1960. R Tourret

Above: **U2 class 4-4-0 No 80 *Dunseverick Castle* waits outside York Road in October 1957. At this angle the similarities between the U2 class and MR 4-4-0s are apparent.** Colour Rail

Above: **On one of the last occasions when steam was used by an Irish railway company, WTs haul a girder train over Bleach Green viaduct on 24th May 1970. The train is on the main line to Londonderry. The lines in the foreground are the up (left) and down Larne lines.** Craig Robb

Right: **Somersault signals at Ballymena. This distinctive type of semaphore was used extensively on the NCC lines and on the CDR narrow gauge.** Derek Young

Above: **Up to 1934 all trains from Belfast to Londonderry had to reverse at Greenisland on the line to Larne, before proceeding north west. A new line was built in the early 1930s to enable these trains to run direct thus eliminating the delays at Greenisland. This involved major engineering works including the viaducts at Bleach Green, seen here and in the top picture on this page. About one third of the finance was provided by the government of Northern Ireland to relieve unemployment but the bulk of the £250,000 required came from the LMS. The now preserved WT tank, No 4, heads a short spoil train along the up Larne line at Bleach Green on 16th March 1967.** Craig Robb

Right: **The advantages of having a large and reasonably prosperous parent was demonstrated by the first large scale introduction of colour light signalling in Ireland, which the LMS installed at York Road in 1926.** Derek Young

Chapter Five

THE NARROW GAUGE

Nothing better illustrates the variety of material that has come to light since the publication of our first colour book, than this chapter. In *Irish Railways in Colour: From Steam to Diesel 1955-1967* we were only able to cover three narrow gauge lines. This time we are able to present colour images of six of the systems, with pictures spanning the period from 1949 until 1961, when the last of Ireland's once extensive network of 3ft gauge lines gave up the fight. In our two volume set *The Irish Narrow Gauge: A Pictorial History*, all of the lines which made up the 500 plus route miles of 3ft gauge track in the country have been covered in a comprehensive manner, with their history and rolling stock discussed in some detail. This brief survey offers the barest of historical background but it may serve to whet the appetites for those who wish to explore this fascinating subject more fully. The colour pictures will also be able to display the liveries used on the various lines in a way in which the monochrome books were unable to do.

THE TRALEE & DINGLE

Above left: **The T&D began operations in March 1891. It linked the county town of Kerry, Tralee, with Dingle, at the end of a peninsula jutting out into the Atlantic. Built on the cheap, with ferocious gradients and long stretches of roadside running as a consequence, the line lost its passenger trains in 1939 but freight services were maintained, after a fashion, until 1953. The last regular working on the line was a monthly cattle train run in connection with the fair in Dingle. The fame of these cattle trains, usually double-headed, spread beyond Ireland and attracted enthusiasts from far afield to record them. On one of the stretches of roadside tramway 2-6-0Ts Nos 1 and 6 are working hard along the grass grown track with one of these cattle specials in the early 1950s.** Colour Rail

Left: **At Annascaul, which was roughly half way between Tralee and Dingle, the cattle trains stopped to take on water. Nos 1 and 6 are again the engines on this occasion.** Colour Rail

THE WEST CLARE RAILWAY

The West Clare ran from Ennis, on the Limerick to Athenry broad gauge line, to twin termini at Kilrush, on the estuary of the River Shannon, and Kilkee on the Atlantic coast of Clare. The line divided at Moyasta Junction. In its early days, a byword for incompetence and the subject of a famous comic song, the West Clare was completely modernised by CIE in the mid-1950s with diesel locomotives and railcars taking over all services.

Above: **A railcar, trailer and van form a service to Ennis at Kilkee in 1957.** Keith Christie

Below: **Colour pictures of West Clare steam locomotives are extremely rare. This view shows No 2, a 2-6-2T tank built by Thomas Green of Leeds in 1900, and withdrawn in 1955 by CIE, approaching Kilrush with a mixed train in June 1953.**
J M Jarvis / Colour Rail

Top: **The railcars were closely based on the last two supplied to the County Donegal system by Walkers in 1950/51. A number of trailers were built by CIE at Inchicore, to run with them. One of the railcars hauling a trailer and van approaches Lahinch in August 1960.**
Cyril Fry / H Stacpoole collection

Above: **As well as the railcars, three Bo-Bo diesel locomotives were supplied by Walkers to eliminate the use of steam on goods trains. These had two powered bogies similar to those used on the railcars. The diesel locos were used on passenger and mixed trains as well as on freights. They had the advantage over the railcars that they did not have to be turned at the termini, the driver having a good**

view in both directions from the elevated centre cab. F503 is leaving Ennistimon in this January 1961 picture. The coach is an ex-Cavan & Leitrim vehicle which was overhauled at Ballinamore in a final flourish of C&L craftsmanship. On the closure of the C&L in 1959 it was sent down to Clare for another few years service. It certainly has a good deal more style than the Inchicore built trailers. John Phillips

Top: **In August 1960 one of the diesels hauls a freight near Lahinch. Most of the Irish narrow gauge lines offered all the services that one would expect from any standard gauge railway. They were proper secondary systems and not just branch feeders or single purpose industrial lines as tended to be the case with the few narrow gauge railways in Britain.** Cyril Fry

Above: **A delightful scene at Miltown Malbay as one of the Walker diesels pauses with a mixed train on 28th January 1961, the year the West Clare, the last surviving narrow gauge line in Ireland, finally closed.** John Phillips

THE CAVAN & LEITRIM RAILWAY

From its opening in the 1880s until closure in March 1959 the C&L was entirely steam operated. Its main line ran from Dromod, on the former MGWR Dublin to Sligo route, north to Belturbet, the terminus of a GNR branch from Ballyhaise on the Clones to Cavan line. There was also a branch off the main line, from the line's headquarters at Ballinamore, to Arigna. The reason for the C&L's survival was to be found at the end of the Arigna branch, where one of Ireland's very few deposits of coal was located. The line to Arigna, always referred to as the tramway, ran for much of the way alongside the public road. Roadside tramways were not uncommon on the continent but rare in these islands. Over the years, as other 3ft gauge lines in the south of Ireland closed down, the GSR and later CIE transferred some of their locomotives and rolling stock to Ballinamore. This variety made the C&L an absolute 'Mecca' for narrow gauge enthusiasts during the 1950s.

Above: **One of the original eight C&L 4-4-0Ts built by Robert Stephenson & Company for the opening of the line in 1887, probably No 8, blows off at Dromod, the line's southern terminus, as it awaits the appointed hour with an evening train to Ballinamore in August 1957.** Midland Publishing collection

Below: **No 6, an ex-Tralee & Dingle 2-6-0T, sent to the C&L in the late 1950s, was the last refugee to find sanctuary there. In the final month of the line's existence, March 1959, No 6 blasts along between Dromod and Dereen.** J G Dewing

Above: **We shall now take a look at some of the engines which worked on the C&L, seen in and around the shed at Ballinamore, starting with one of the C&L 4-4-0Ts No 2, originally named** *Kathleen*, **now preserved at the Ulster Folk and Transport Museum at Cultra, near Belfast. No 2 has been largely unaltered over the years, retaining her original dome and chimney.** Keith Christie

Above right: **Two former T&D engines are on shed. No 4, on the left, a 1903 built Kerr Stuart 2-6-0T, was moved to Ballinamore in 1941 by the GSR. In the foreground is No 6, a Hunslet 2-6-0T dating from 1898, which was overhauled at Inchicore and sent to the C&L in 1957 to cope with an upsurge in coal traffic at that time. This picture was taken on 17th June 1958.** Midland Publishing collection

Below: **A general view of the shed yard taken from Ballinamore's station footbridge, the only one on the C&L! Nearest the camera is T&D No 4. On the adjacent track are C&L 4-4-0 No 3, T&D 2-6-2T No 5 and another unidentified 4-4-0T. Beyond the coal and ash wagons is T&D 2-6-0T No 3.**
Midland Publishing collection

Above: No 10 was one of four 2-4-2Ts built in 1900 by Neilson Reid, which constituted the entire fleet of the the Cork, Blackrock & Passage Railway. When this line was closed in 1932 by the GSR, all four were sent to Ballinamore. Designed for the relatively high speeds of the Cork line's suburban services and with driving wheels of 4ft 6in diameter, at first sight they seemed unsuited to the C&L. Restricted to the Belturbet to Dromod section, their wheels being too big to cope with the sharp curves on the tramway, they nevertheless gave years of sterling service on the C&L with two of them, Nos 12 and 10, lasting until closure in 1959.
Midland Publishing collection

Below: No 3, one of the three 2-6-0Ts supplied by Hunslet for the opening of the Tralee & Dingle line in 1891, came north in 1941 and is seen shunting at Ballinamore in June 1958. This was one of two No 3s at work on the line at this time, the other being a 4-4-0T.
Midland Publishing collection

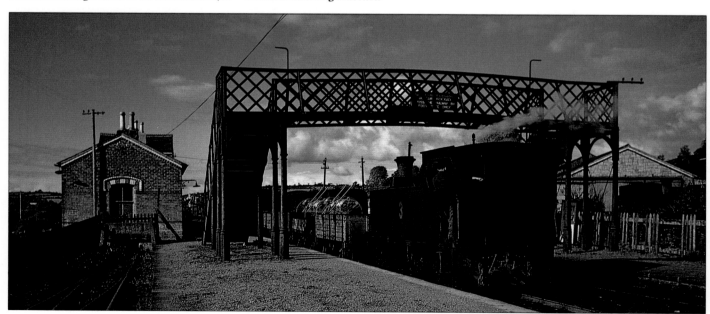

Right: **Heading north east from Ballinamore, ex-CB&P No 10 pauses at Bawnboy Road with the daily train which conveyed passengers on this section.** Midland Publishing collection

Below centre: **2-4-2T No 10 receives lubrication and water during a stop at Ballyconnell on 29th July 1957. A train of coal empties bound for Ballinamore is in the loop. In the 1950s it took 3 hours to cover the 33 miles from Dromod to Belturbet, hardly breakneck speed, even by the modest standards of the Irish narrow gauge.** A D Hutchinson

Bottom: **No 10 is ready to leave Belturbet. The GNR connecting service to Ballyhaise is at the far end of other platform. The narrow gauge train terminated at Ballinamore where passengers for Dromod would have had to wait up to 1½ hours for a connecting service over the southern part of the line.** A D Hutchinson

THE ARIGNA TRAMWAY

Top: **No survey of the C&L would be complete without reference to the branch from Ballinamore to Arigna. T&D No 3 heads the daily** mixed train with passenger accommodation being provided in one of the original C&L clerestory coaches which dated from the opening of the line. Keith Christie

Above: **T&D 2-6-0 No 3 takes water at Drumshanbo on its way to Arigna in the summer of** 1958. Drumshanbo, 12 miles from Ballinamore and 3 miles from Arigna, was the only community of any size served by the tramway. Without the coal traffic from the pits above Arigna it is unlikely the line would have survived as long as it did.
Midland Publishing collection

Top: An extension beyond Arigna station up to the mines was opened as late as 1920. Part of this, to the original terminus at Aughabehy closed as early as 1927. It was the pits at Derreenavoggy, 4¼ miles from Arigna, which provided the coal traffic for the railway. The 1920 extension never had a passenger service. T&D

No 3 brings a loaded coal train down from the mines over the level crossing near Arigna station on 2nd September 1957. Keith Walton

Above: When the Irish government decided to build a coal-fired power station near Arigna the *raison d'être* for the railway disappeared,

though coal continued to be shipped out over the railway to the cement factories of Drogheda and Limerick for a while after the power station opened in 1957. A train of Arigna coal heads along the tramway on 17th August 1957 seemingly ignored by a more traditional Irish form of transport. Midland Publishing collection

THE LONDONDERRY & LOUGH SWILLY RAILWAY

At its peak the L&LSR operated the second largest narrow gauge system in Ireland with 99 route miles of track. This had begun to contract as early as 1935 with the closure of the line from Buncrana to Carndonagh. The line from Letterkenny to Burtonport closed in June 1940, though part of the route, to Gweedore, was reopened from March 1941 until January 1947 for freight, due to wartime shortages of oil for the replacement road services. By 1950 just the lines from Londonderry to Letterkenny and Buncrana remained open for freight and in the case of the latter, the occasional excursion during the summer. The company abandoned rail services completely in 1953. Our pictures were taken on the Buncrana line in July 1950 by A D Hutchinson.

Top left: **A train arrives at Fahan on the shores of Lough Swilly headed by No 10. From here a ferry plied across the lough to Rathmullan.**

Top right: **No 10 waits at Fahan station with a train from Londonderry for Buncrana.**

Above: **4-6-2T No 10, one of a pair built by Kerr Stuart in 1904 and originally named *Richmond*, runs round its train at Buncrana. Its sister locomotive was withdrawn as early as 1928.**

COUNTY DONEGAL
RAILWAY

Top: It seems logical to begin our coverage of Ireland's largest and finest narrow gauge railway at Letterkenny. The CDR branch from Strabane was opened as late as 1909 and was largely paid for by the joint owners of the CDR, the MR and the GNR. The CDR terminus was adjacent to the L&LSR through station on their line from Derry to Burtonport. This pointless duplication of facilities was typical of the lack of co-operation between County Donegal's two narrow gauge railways over the years. The CDR station is to the left and that of the L&LSR on the right. The blue and cream half cab bus was operated by the GNR. This worked the route, instigated in the late 1940s by the CDR general manager B L Curran, between Letterkenny and Ballybofey. The journey by rail between these towns was circuitous and would have involved a change at Strabane. The other bus was owned by the L&LSR which, while it continued in existence as a bus and lorry operator long after its trains had ceased to run, still kept the word 'railway' in its title. Keith Walton

Above: In May 1959 CDR class 5 2-6-4T No 5 *Drumboe* brings a Letterkenny to Strabane freight over the abandoned trackbed of the L&LSR line to Tooban Junction and Derry, just beyond Letterkenny station. J G Dewing

COUNTY DONEGAL STEAM

Opposite page top left: **Three classes of CDR steam locomotive could still be seen in the 1950s. No 11 Erne was the last survivor of four 4-6-4 or Baltic tanks built by Nasmyth Wilson in 1904. This was the last locomotive of this wheel arrangement in the British Isles. Tragically and shortsightedly it was cut up in 1967.** Keith Christie

Opposite page top right: **The rest of the steam fleet was made up of two classes of 2-6-4 tanks all built by Nasmyth Wilson between 1907 and 1912. Class 5 2-6-4T No 4 Meenglas was recorded outside the shed at Strabane.** Keith Christie

Opposite page centre: **The CDR's last steam locomotives, the class 5As, represented here by No 2 Blanche seen shunting at Stranorlar, were a development of the earlier 2-6-4Ts. The most obvious difference between the two types was the larger tanks of the later engines.** Keith Bannister

Opposite page bottom: **In the yard at Strabane railcar No 12 which dated from 1936, coupled to a pair of trailers, awaits its next turn, as No 6 Columbkille shunts wagons up to the trans-shipment shed where freight was exchanged with the GNR broad gauge line.** A D Hutchinson

STRABANE

Below: **The CDR's only diesel locomotive Phoenix, numbered 11 in the railcar series, was invariably to be found bustling wagons around at Strabane. It began life as a steam tractor on the Clogher Valley Railway. As built it was apparently underpowered and virtually useless. The CDR's manager Henry Forbes purchased the machine for 100 guineas and had it successfully transformed into a diesel shunter at Dundalk. The canny Forbes is supposed to have sold its old boiler to a laundry. When the CDR closed, Phoenix was secured for preservation and can now be seen in the**

transport gallery of the Ulster Folk and Transport Museum at Cultra, just outside Belfast. The broad gauge loco in this 1959 picture is U class 4-4-0 No 65, the former GNR No 200, *Lough Melvin*, one of two engines of this name which the UTA possessed at this time, the other being the former SLNCR 0-6-4 tank. Keith Bannister

Bottom: **Class 5 2-6-4 tank, No 4 Meenglas positions coach No 58, built in 1928 for the narrow gauge boat trains which ran on the LMS NCC line from Larne to Ballymena, at the front of the goods to Donegal Town. Members of the Irish Railway Record Society travelled in the coach on an outing on 22nd June 1959.** Michael Costeloe

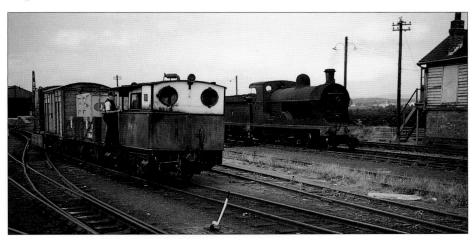

RAILCARS

Opposite page top: **The first of the Walker railcars supplied to an Irish railway was this one, which went to the Clogher Valley Railway in 1932. Henry Forbes, the CDR manager, was on that line's committee of management, so it is fair to surmise that the success of this diesel railcar there, was the catalyst which led to similar types being acquired by the CDR. Bought by the CDR on the closure of the Clogher Valley in 1941, railcar 10 was the smallest in the CDR fleet with a seating capacity for 28 passengers. This historic vehicle has found a suitable resting place at the Ulster Folk and Transport Museum.** Keith Bannister

Opposite page bottom: **The final development of the Walker railcar came with Nos 19 and 20 in 1950/51. Compare this picture of No 19 at Killybegs taken on 17th October 1956 with that on the page opposite when it had the more elaborate front end livery. The other point of interest in the picture is the turntable at Killybegs, made with typical CDR economy, from the frames of a scrapped tank locomotive.** Michael Costello

STRANORLAR

Top left and top right: **Two unusual views of the power unit of a CDR railcar without its passenger saloon attached. Railcar No 12 was the first of the Walker diesel railcars supplied new to the CDR. The 1934-built unit was having some attention at the works when recorded in this state of undress by Keith Bannister.**

Above left: **The CDR's works and headquarters were at Stranorlar. Class 5A *Blanche* was receiving a repaint and some repairs when recorded outside the works. This locomotive can be seen today at the Ulster Folk and Transport Museum at Cultra.** Keith Christie

Bottom right: **In 1930 the CDR introduced what is believed to have been the first diesel powered railcar in the British Isles. This vehicle, No 7, had a 30-seat body, was powered by a Gardner diesel engine and was finally withdrawn in 1949. From this relatively unsophisticated machine, illustrated on page 94 of Midland Publishing's book *The Irish Narrow Gauge – A Pictorial History: volume 2*, the whole family of CDR railcars evolved. Seen at Stranorlar on 10th September 1954 is the penultimate CDR Walker railcar, No 19, built in 1950 and still in existence today on the Isle of Man Railway. For some years in the early 1950s No 19 ran with this rather ornate front end paint scheme, although this was later replaced by plain red up to the panel where the number was located.** R Tourret

Top: **Railcar No 18, a 43-seater built in 1940 and rebuilt after a fire in 1949, has recently been lovingly restored to full working order at the Foyle Valley Railway Museum, on the site of the old GNR station at Foyle Road in Derry (see page 80). No 18 is seen here at Friary Halt near Rossnowlagh on the only all year round** scheduled Sunday morning CDR working, which conveyed worshippers to the nearby Franciscan Friary from Ballyshannon. The railcar was turned at Rossnowlagh on the turntable which had formerly been at the CDR's station at Victoria Road in Londonderry. If the plans of the South Donegal Railway Restoration Society come to fruition, 3ft gauge trains may return to part of the Ballyshannon branch of the CDR. John Langford

Above: **Railcar No 16, a 41 seater built in 1936, was also powered by a Gardner diesel engine. It is seen at Letterkenny, 1959.** Keith Bannister

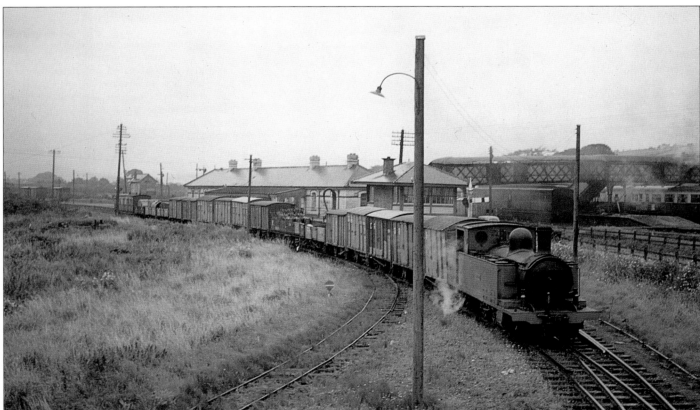

Top: **Whilst the CDR had used diesel railcars successfully for many years on regular passenger services, the line's fleet of carriages were kept in good order and were put to use on special trains and excursions. On one of these, a special from Strabane to Ballyshannon, No 2 *Blanche* arrives at Lough Eske sta-** tion on 4th August 1958. Keith Walton

Above: **The steam fleet was used for the CDR's healthy freight traffic. Here class 5A 2-6-4T No 2 *Blanche* is about to depart from Strabane with a goods train to Letterkenny in August 1958. The departure of this train and many** other memorable CDR sequences are to be found on our video programme *Irish Railways volume 3: The Irish Narrow Gauge, Colour Films 1939-1959.* Keith Christie

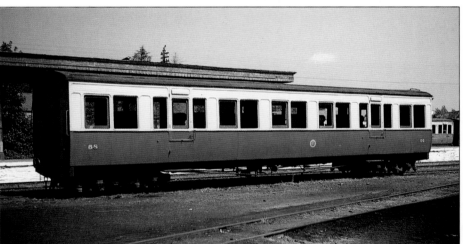

Above: **In respect of their braking systems CDR goods wagons, and indeed the great majority of such vehicles used on the Irish 3ft gauge lines, were superior to those operating on the standard gauge railways of Britain and Ireland, in that they had continuous vacuum brakes. Instead of heavy ballasted brake vans at the end of goods trains the CDR usually had one of these bogie passenger brake coaches to accommodate the guard and the odd passenger, who was not deterred by the long stops for shunting at intermediate stations. Here the brake coach off the Letterkenny goods has been abandoned while the train shunts at Raphoe.** Keith Christie

Centre: **CDR Coach No 58, formerly LMS NCC No 318, was built at York Road in Belfast in 1928, using the underframe of a much older vehicle dating back to 1879. With corridor connections, electric light and steam heating, this and two other coaches built at the same time were for use on Larne to Ballymena boat trains. When passenger services ended on this line in 1933, the coaches found further service on the Ballycastle line, being sold to the CDR by the UTA when that, the final part of the narrow gauge in County Antrim, closed in 1950. By the time they reached Stranorlar the corridor connections had been dispensed with. They were the longest and widest carriages on the system, as befitted probably the finest passenger coaches ever used on the Irish narrow gauge.** Keith Bannister

Bottom: **Numbered in their own sequence, separate from both carriages and wagons, were the 'red vans', a term used officially to describe some lighter than normal goods wagons, which were to run exclusively with the railcars. Nos 15 and 18, seen here at Strabane, came to the CDR from the Clogher Valley Railway when it closed in 1941.** Michael Costeloe

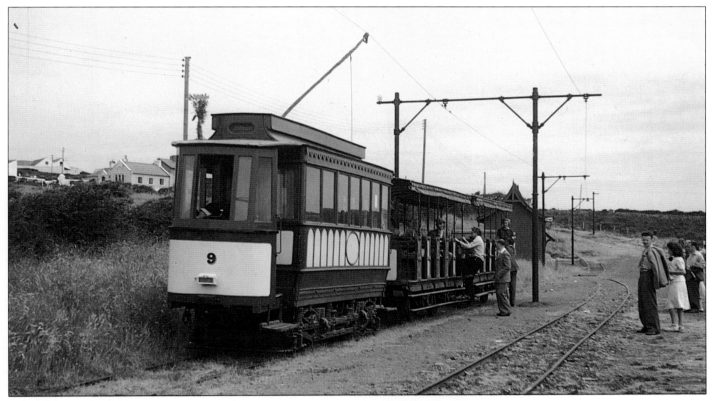

THE GIANT'S CAUSEWAY TRAMWAY

To conclude our chapter on the narrow gauge and make a bridge to the next one, I am delighted to be able to include these remarkably good pictures of one of the most historically significant 3ft gauge lines in Ireland, which closed as early as 1949. When it opened in 1883 the GCT provided the first serious application of hydro electricity for railway or tramway operation in these islands. At first, power was drawn from a third rail beside the track but in 1899 the line was converted to conventional current collection from an overhead wire.

The tramway ran for about 8 miles along the scenic North Antrim coast from the seaside resort of Portrush to Bushmills, a place venerated by discerning whiskey drinkers, and from there on to the strange basalt rock formations at the Giant's Causeway, which is one of Ireland's foremost tourist attractions. Lack of funds to renew the line and a lack of interest from the UTA and the Philistines who governed Northern Ireland at that time, forced the directors of the line to close it at the end of September 1949. How short-sighted this was: what a tourist attraction it would be if it were still open today.

We are fortunate that A D Hutchinson visited the line in July 1949 to record these scenes which were soon to be history.

Top right: **A 'toast rack' tram hauling two trailers, its identity unfortunately obscured by the gentlemen in front of it, pauses at a request stop near Portrush.**

Top left: **On the final stretch between Bushmills and the Causeway, the tramway passed over the River Bush on the Victoria Jubilee bridge.**

Above: **Passengers join a tram and a trailer at the Giant's Causeway terminus. Car No 9 was delivered as an unpowered trailer in the 1890s and converted to a powered tramcar in 1909. It was normal practice to run open and closed vehicles in the same formation so that passengers had a choice of accommodation depending on the weather.**

RAILWAY BUS SERVICES

& TRAMWAYS

GNR BUSES

The Great Northern Railway which ran bus services for many years, feeding passengers into the railway network, was attempting to run an integrated transport system, a concept often sneered at today, but one which will have to come back into favour if we are to avoid covering the whole of the planet in tarmac. It was forced to sell its buses in Northern Ireland to the Northern Ireland Road Transport Board in the 1930s and despite assurances to the contrary, the Board began to run buses in competition with the trains rather than as the GNR had done, using the buses to provide feeder services. The GNR continued to run bus services in the south of Ireland up to 1958, when they were taken over by CIE.

Above right: **AEC double decker No 304 was delivered new to the GNR in 1953. It had seats for 36 on the upper deck and 30 downstairs. It is seen here at Howth working on a route which the company had taken over from a private operator in 1929. The service ran from Eden Quay in the city centre through Fairview, Raheny and Sutton to a terminus at the East Pier in Howth. The timetable issued in November 1929 for the service displays bus times in light type and trains in bold. Return tickets were valid on either the buses or trains on the Howth branch. When CIE took over the GNR service it became route 31 in their Dublin City services. Since the Howth line was electrified, the importance and frequency of this particular bus route has declined.**
John Edgington

Bottom right: **GNR single decker No 367, seen at Enniskillen station in the summer of 1957, was built in 1949 and withdrawn by CIE in 1962. Though banned from operating services within Northern Ireland, GNR buses entered the province on services from the Republic. This bus was employed on the route from Enniskillen to Cavan via Belturbet.**
Midland Publishing collection

FROM RAILS TO ROAD

Top: **When the CDR stopped running train services, like the Lough Swilly before them, they continued to operate road services (see page 79). Here, on 29th August 1960, are some of the buses which took over the former railway passenger services. On the platform at Strabane from which CDR trains used to depart,** on the right bearing a CDR logo, is one of the six P class single-deckers hired by the CDR from CIE, to work the routes formerly served by their trains. P30 built in 1948 and withdrawn by CIE in 1962, is on a service to Letterkenny. The CIE bus on the left is destined for Killybegs. Michael Costeloe

Above: **This was how the former L&LSR railway station at Letterkenny looked in 1958. Swilly road freight vehicles are on the trackbed and** next to the GNR-built bus, now in CIE livery, to the left of the picture, is a Lough Swilly one. Still officially a railway company, though one without track or trains, the L&LSR logo on the open door of the Bedford lorry is similar to the device applied to locomotives in the final years of railway operations. A signal in the 'off' position can just be seen on the CDR line to the left of the red tanker. The two stations were, of course, beside each other (see page 115). Keith Bannister

TRAMS & BUSES IN BELFAST

Top: **The Ulster Transport Authority which took over the LMS NCC and the Belfast & County Down system in 1948 and the remaining GNR lines in 1958 was also the operator of the province's bus services. The pre-occupation of the UTA and its political masters with road transport resulted in the destruction of most of Northern Ireland's railway network by 1965. A pair of UTA Leyland double-deckers in the Authority's attractive two-tone** green and white livery is seen at the Oxford Street bus station in Belfast around 1965.
Midland Publishing collection

Above: **Belfast Corporation Tramways were unusual in that they ran on tracks with a gauge of 4ft 9in. The story of Belfast's trams is typical of many of the municipal tramway systems in Britain. Plans for the abandonment of the trams were laid before the war. In the case of Belfast they were to be replaced with trolleybuses but these could not be obtained because of wartime shortages and this gave some tram routes a stay of execution. The last** trams finally ran in 1954. Our views show the two types of tramcars that remained in service until the end. Both of these were named after the General Managers of the system at the time of their introduction. One of Belfast's tram routes terminated inside the erstwhile Belfast & County Down Railway station at Queen's Quay, providing a convenient interchange for passengers. There was only a single track line for the last few yards into the station, which Chamberlain car No 342 is seen here negotiating in September 1953, at the end of a journey from Ligoniel in the north of the city. This tramcar was the first of a batch of 50 new 33ft long vehicles introduced in 1930. No 342 was built by the Brush Engineering Company Limited at Slough. W E Robertson / Colour Rail

Opposite page top: **Later that day Chamberlain car No 389 is seen leaving Queen's Quay station bound for Ligoniel, as McCreary car No 423 waits outside the station for the outgoing car to clear the single track section.**
W E Robertson / Colour Rail

Opposite page bottom: **No 421 was a McCreary streamline car built by English Electric at Preston in 1935, one of a batch of 50 which were Belfast's last new tramcars. Some of the trolleybuses which replaced the trams and are now themselves but a memory, can be seen in the background. No 421 was photographed in Donegall Square North in 1953, the year before the system was finally abandoned.**
A D Hutchinson

THE HILL OF HOWTH TRAMWAY

The Hill of Howth Tramway ran from 1901 until 1959. Built to the Irish standard gauge, it was 5¼ miles in length, single track with passing loops and connected the railway stations at Sutton and Howth on the GNR branch off the Dublin to Belfast main line from Howth Junction, about 5 miles out from Amiens Street station. Built and operated by the GNR the tramway was popular with visitors and tourists, offering as it did access to the picturesque Hill of Howth some 560 feet above sea level and giving superb views over the wide expanse of Dublin Bay. The tramway also served the residents of the Hill throughout the year.

Above: **Eight tramcars were built for the opening of the line by the Brush Electrical Company at Loughborough. They ran on two Brill trucks and seated 30 inside and 37 on top. Car Nos 1 and 7 are filling up at Howth station on a sunny summer Sunday in August 1957, which today sees electric traction once again as the northern terminus of the Dublin Area Rapid Transit, commonly known as 'the Dart'.**
F W Shuttleworth

Below: **Car Nos 2 and 7 cross at the summit in August 1957.** Midland Publishing collection

Above: **In August 1958 tramcar No 4 coasts down hill towards Howth with its trolley pole intentionally off the wires to save wear, as the conductor collects the fares on the top deck.** Midland Publishing collection

Below: **The trolley pole on car No 6 is reversed by the conductor at Sutton ready for the journey back over the hill to Howth, in August 1958.** Midland Publishing collection

THE FINTONA HORSE TRAM

The GNR's other tramway was very different to that operated between Howth and Sutton. The famous Fintona horse tram ran from the 1850s until 1957 along the ¾ mile branch, between Fintona Junction, on the Omagh to Enniskillen line, and the village of Fintona. The tramcar dated from 1883 and had accommodation for all three classes.

Above: **On 22nd August 1957 the horse which pulled the tram is led to his shed at Fintona Junction where he was always put before the connecting services arrived, as it seems he did not take kindly to noisy steam locomotives.** Although the horses changed over the years, and were geldings not mares as suggested in the previous volume, they were always given the name 'Dick'. Midland Publishing collection

Below: Dick and the tram are ready to leave Fintona for the Junction in July 1957. Tramcar No 381 is now displayed at the Ulster Folk and Transport Museum at Cultra. A D Hutchinson

130

Chapter Seven

INDUSTRIAL RAILWAYS

Ireland never had much in the way of the heavy industry which was so common in parts of Britain. The lack of significant deposits of coal and iron ore meant that the industrial revolution never really happened in Ireland. As a consequence of this the prevalence of industrial railways was not very great. However some interesting systems which survived into the 1950s and '60s are recorded on the following pages.

Above: **As WT class 2-6-4T No 3 storms through Mount station near Carrickfergus, with a boat train from Larne Harbour to Belfast York Road on Saturday 2nd October 1965, in the exchange sidings to the right of the picture can be seen one of the two Peckett-built saddle tanks which were employed at the large Courtaulds factory, which was situated here.** Craig Robb

Right: **The two Pecketts were *Patricia* (works number 2088 of 1948), and *Wilfrid* (2113 of 1950). They were used to take wagons of coal, delivered by rail from the docks at Belfast, into the plant. The locomotives were active until the mid-1960s, when they were offered for sale in advertisements in the local papers. Sadly no one came to save them and these unusual 5ft 3in gauge Pecketts were scrapped. Colour films of the saddle tanks in action, made by John Laird, who also took this photograph, appear on our video *Irish Railways volume 4: Twilight of Steam in Ulster*.**

Above: **British Aluminium opened a plant at Larne in 1900 and for many years operated a 3ft gauge railway to convey both coal and materials around the site. The system was worked by three delightful little Peckett 0-4-0 tank locomotives. No 1, works number 1026 of 1904, was privately preserved when the line closed, and worked for a number of years on the now defunct Shane's Castle Railway near Antrim.** Colour Rail

Below: **The Londonderry Port & Harbour Commissioners operated the railways along the quays at Derry, which provided a tenuous link between the city's four railway stations. The quayside lines were of mixed gauge so that both broad and narrow gauge wagons could run on them. The LP&HC operated a number of locomotives since 1867, when these lines were first used. No 1 was built by Robert Stephenson & Company in 1891 and is now** preserved at Cultra. **The LP&HC engines were 5ft 3in gauge themselves, although they could haul wagons of either gauge and were equipped with two sets of draw gear. This 1963 picture of the locomotive standing on the mixed gauge track outside her shed, clearly shows the conventional hook and three link coupling for broad gauge wagons and the extended hook-come-buffer used with narrow gauge stock.** Des FitzGerald

BELFAST DOCK LINES

Opposite page top: **The once extensive network of dock lines at Belfast provided a link between the LMS NCC system at York Road and the GNR and B&CDR via the former Belfast Central Railway at East Bridge Street Junction. Here, ex-GNR PG class No 10 heads a goods train from York Road along the quays on 15th May 1962.** Richard Whitford

Opposite page bottom: **Locomotive coal for Great Northern sheds was always delivered to Abercorn Basin on the County Down side of the River Lagan whilst supplies for the NCC lines were landed at Albert Quay on the County Antrim side. Even though both sections were under the control of the UTA after 1958, separate coal deliveries continued to the end of steam. An ex-GNR U class 4-4-0 was at Abercorn Basin to collect wagons of loco coal on a misty Autumn morning in 1965.** Craig Robb

THE ULTIMATE TANK

Top: One of the oddest sights ever to appear on Irish railway tracks was surely this surprising combination, which those underrated Einsteins of the UTA unleashed in 1965. The idea was simple, how do you get a 'Jeep' to Dublin without having to take water en route? The startling simplicity of their answer was to shove an old NCC tender on the back. The only problem was that the locomotive's injectors were not able to bring the water through from the tender and worse still, to compound this, on uphill stretches, water from the side tanks flowed into the tender. Come back Mr Bulleid et Monsieur Lartigue, all is forgiven! The failure of the concept at least meant that railway enthusiasts did not have to invent a new name for this combination of a tank locomotive with a tender. On one of its few outings in this condition, WT class No 55 and friend are on their way from Adelaide shed to Great Victoria Street to work a cross border service on 18th May 1965.

Above: No 55 and tender head for Dublin passing Belfast Central Junction later the same day. Both Midland Publishing collection

OOPS!

Left: **We have all heard of the phrase 'off road Jeep', as applied to motor vehicles. This is what that expression meant to railwaymen in Ulster in the days of steam. No 8 was the culprit at Adelaide on 13th June 1964.**

Centre: **On Wednesday 5th April 1967 the afternoon 'perishables' van train from Larne Harbour to Belfast York Road came to grief near Ballycarry with the consequences seen here. The train, hauled by a pair of multi-purpose diesel units, consisted of a number of the vacuum braked vans, with a brand new spoil wagon bringing up the rear. These vehicles had a reputation for instability when empty and it was probably the wagon which first derailed itself before bringing the vans off the track. The 'perishables' lived up to its name that afternoon, the contents of several vans finishing up in the Lough.**

Bottom left: **On 18th February 1967 the former SLNCR 0-6-4 tank, No 27 *Lough Erne*, bought by the UTA when its own line closed in 1957, was derailed over the ash pit at York Road running shed with the alarming consequences seen here. No 27 was soon back at work and at the end of its UTA service it was bought for preservation – a suitable conclusion to the career of the last conventional steam locomotive supplied to an Irish railway.**

Opposite page bottom: **After the end of the spoil contract there was little left for the remaining 'Jeeps' to do. On two Sundays in May 1970 they were entrusted with the last major job for steam in Ireland when a total of eight large steel girders for motorway bridges were conveyed from York Road to Ballyclare Junction. No 4 heads the first of these workings near Monkstown on 24th May 1970, on her way to bringing the curtain down on the age of steam in Ireland.**

THE SWANSONG OF STEAM

When Northern Ireland Railways was formed in 1968, it inherited 22 steam locomotives from the UTA. One of the reasons for the retention of some of the 'Jeeps' was the contract which the railway won to transport quarry spoil from Magheramorne, between Whitehead and Larne, to the shores of Belfast Lough outside York Road. The spoil was used to reclaim the land on which the M2 Motorway was later built. The spoil trains – over 7,600 of them in total – ran from November 1966 to May 1970. Various formations were tried, the most common was 20 wagons with a loco at each end, which made for a train of over 900 tons in weight. The specially designed 4-wheel wagons had hydraulically operated side doors, and were built by Cravens. The spoil trains had to climb the 4½ mile Greenisland bank, with a ruling gradient of 1 in 98, on their way to Belfast. The sound of two 'Jeeps' hard at work on the bank was a memorable one. Regular steam workings in Ireland ended in a quite spectacular way on these trains.

Top: **On Monday 17th June 1968 a double headed spoil train has almost reached the top of Greenisland bank. The train was recorded a few hundred yards on the Carrickfergus side of Greenisland station. Pilot locomotive No 55 seems to be doing most of the work.**

Centre: **The now preserved WT No 4 heads a spoil train which demonstrates the more normal method of working with an engine at each end. The train is passing through the staggered platforms of Barn station near Carrickfergus, on 16th March 1967.**

All photographs on pages 142 / 143 by Craig Robb